PORTFOLIO PENGUIN

TAX-FREE SAVINGS ACCOUNTS

GORDON PAPE is Canada's best-known financial author and the publisher of three investment newsletters: *The Income Investor*, *The Canada Report*, and *The Internet Wealth Builder*. He is the author of several national bestsellers, including *Retirement's Harsh New Realities* and *Sleep-Easy Investing*. He has spoken at hundreds of seminars in Canada and the United States, is frequently quoted in the media, and is a popular guest on radio and television shows. His website is located at www. BuildingWealth.ca.

Also by Gordon Pape

INVESTMENT ADVICE

Money Savvy Kids
(with Deborah Kerbel)
Retirement's Harsh New Realities
The Ultimate TFSA Guide
Tax-Free Savings Accounts
Sleep-Easy Investing
The Retirement Time Bomb
Get Control of Your Money
6 Steps to $1 Million
Retiring Wealthy in the 21st Century
The Complete Guide to RRIFs and LIFs
(with David Tafler)
Gordon Pape's 2004 Buyer's Guide to
Mutual Funds (with Eric Kirzner)
Gordon Pape's 2004 Buyer's Guide to
RRSPs

Secrets of Successful Investing
(with Eric Kirzner)
Gordon Pape's Investing Strategies 2001
(with Richard Croft and Eric Kirzner)
Making Money in Mutual Funds
The Canadian Mortgage Book
(with Bruce McDougall)
The Best of Pape's Notes
Head Start (with Frank Jones)
Retiring Wealthy
Building Wealth in the '90s
Low-Risk Investing in the '90s
Low-Risk Investing
Building Wealth

CONSUMER ADVICE

Gordon Pape's International Shopping Advice (with Deborah Kerbel)

HUMOUR

The $50,000 Stove Handle

CHRISTMAS (with Deborah Kerbel)

Quizmas Carols
Family Quizmas
Quizmas: Christmas Trivia Family Fun
(www.quizmas.net)

FICTION (with Tony Aspler)

Chain Reaction
The Scorpion Sanction
The Music Wars

NON-FICTION

Montreal at the Crossroads (with Donna Gabeline and Dane Lanken)

Tax-Free Savings Accounts

How TFSAs Can Make You **Rich**

Gordon Pape

PORTFOLIO
PENGUIN

PORTFOLIO PENGUIN
an imprint of Penguin Canada

Published by the Penguin Group
Penguin Group (Canada), 90 Eglinton Avenue East, Suite 700, Toronto, Ontario, Canada M4P 2Y3

Penguin Group (USA) Inc., 375 Hudson Street, New York, New York 10014, U.S.A.
Penguin Books Ltd, 80 Strand, London WC2R 0RL, England
Penguin Ireland, 25 St Stephen's Green, Dublin 2, Ireland (a division of Penguin Books Ltd)
Penguin Group (Australia), 707 Collins Street, Melbourne, Victoria 3008, Australia
    (a division of Pearson Australia Group Pty Ltd)
Penguin Books India Pvt Ltd, 11 Community Centre, Panchsheel Park, New Delhi – 110 017, India
Penguin Group (NZ), 67 Apollo Drive, Rosedale, Auckland 0632, New Zealand
    (a division of Pearson New Zealand Ltd)
Penguin Books (South Africa) (Pty) Ltd, 24 Sturdee Avenue, Rosebank,
    Johannesburg 2196, South Africa

Penguin Books Ltd, Registered Offices: 80 Strand, London WC2R 0RL, England

First published 2013

1 2 3 4 5 6 7 8 9 10 (WEB)

Copyright © Gordon Pape Enterprises Ltd., 2013

This publication contains the opinions and ideas of its author and is designed to provide useful advice in regard to the subject matter covered. The author and publisher are not engaged in rendering legal, accounting, or other professional services in this publication. This publication is not intended to provide a basis for action in particular circumstances without consideration by a competent professional. The author and publisher expressly disclaim any responsibility for any liability, loss, or risk, personal or otherwise, which is incurred as a consequence, directly or indirectly, of the use and application of any of the contents of this book.

Manufactured in Canada.

LIBRARY AND ARCHIVES CANADA CATALOGUING IN PUBLICATION

Pape, Gordon, 1936–
Tax-Free Saving Accounts : how TFSAs can make you rich / Gordon Pape.

Includes bibliographical references and index.

ISBN 978-0-14-318477-5

1. Tax-Free Savings Accounts (Canada). 2. Finance, Personal—Canada.
3. Saving and investment—Canada. 4. Tax planning—Canada. I. Title.

HG179.P3767 2013   332.024'010971   C2012-907026-2

Visit the Penguin Canada website at www.penguin.ca

Special and corporate bulk purchase rates available; please see
www.penguin.ca/corporatesales or call 1-800-810-3104, ext. 2477.

ALWAYS LEARNING   PEARSON

To Shirley:
Still my one true love after fifty years of marriage.
—*Gordon*

Contents

Introduction

This is the third edition of this book. The original was written in the fall of 2008 at which time Tax-Free Savings Accounts had not even been officially launched and most people knew very little about them. As a result, some of the information in that book was later overtaken by events and by changes in government rules and interpretations.

By the time the expanded version, called *The Ultimate TFSA Guide*, appeared in 2010, many of the teething problems had been ironed out. But it was clear that many Canadians still did not understand exactly how the plans worked, how to use them effectively, or the potentially serious ramifications of using them improperly.

The situation had not improved much by mid-2012. That was apparent in the findings of a CIBC survey published in August of that year. The bank found that, although an encouraging 44 percent of Canadians have opened a TFSA, fewer than half of those people had actually made a contribution to the plan that year. And when asked what they intended to do with any money in their plan, 41 percent said they had no idea!

TFSAs look simple at first glance. You deposit money into an account and later withdraw it tax-free to use however you wish. Just like bank savings accounts, some might say.

Except they're not! TFSAs are much more complex than they first appear, as proven by the hundreds of questions I have received since the original *Tax-Free Savings Accounts* was published in early 2009.

Tens of thousands of Canadians discovered just how tricky TFSAs can be when they received notices from the Canada Revenue Agency (CRA) in 2010 and 2011 telling them they had overcontributed to their accounts and would have to pay penalties that in some cases amounted to several hundred dollars. The problem was simply a misunderstanding of the rules, and the CRA eventually decided to be lenient with those who had made honest mistakes. But that tolerance won't last forever.

Some of the key elements of the program have evolved since the plan was originally unveiled by Finance Minister Jim Flaherty in his 2008 budget. The CRA has interpreted some of the tax rules differently than originally envisaged by the Department of Finance. Issues relating to the cross-border treatment of the plans and their status under the Canada–U.S. Tax Treaty have created some potential pitfalls for investors. Rules relating to such transactions as swaps have been changed. Financial institutions have launched a wide range of plans, in some cases leaving people confused about what they can and can't invest in.

This revised and updated edition addresses all these topics and provides up-to-date answers. You'll also find a wide range of TFSA questions from readers with my answers.

If after digesting all this information you are still uncertain about something, send your own question to me at Gordon. Pape@BuildingWealth.ca and type "TFSA book question" in the subject line. I can't provide personal answers, but replies to selected questions will be posted on www.Building Wealth.ca.

Tax-Free Savings Accounts are a great way to build personal wealth but they need to be used properly. I hope this new edition will help you to achieve that.

1
The Beginning: Budget 2008

No one expected much when Finance Minister Jim Flaherty stood up to give his Budget Speech in the House of Commons at four o'clock on February 26, 2008.

The cupboard was pretty much bare. The Conservative government, anticipating an early election, had dipped deeply into the nation's dwindling surplus the previous October, when Flaherty had delivered an Economic Statement that was actually a mini-budget in very thin disguise.

At that time, the finance minister announced a second cut in the Goods and Services Tax (GST), reducing it to 5 percent, as the Tories had promised during their election campaign. And that was just the beginning. Mr. Flaherty unveiled a reduction of half a percentage point in the lowest-tier income tax rate, increased personal tax exemptions across the board for all Canadians, cut the rates on Employment Insurance, and announced deep cuts to the federal corporate tax rate, slashing it from 22.1 percent to 15 percent by 2012.

The total cost of all those tax goodies was estimated at a whopping $188.1 billion over the next six fiscal years. Of that, $72.7 billion was eaten up by the GST cut, $64.9 billion went to income tax savings, and $50.5 billion to the corporate tax cuts.

But after handing out all those goodies, the Conservatives discovered the opposition parties were in no mood to force an election. Instead, they went along with every measure presented to them by the government, thwarting Stephen Harper's plans for an early election.

That left the government with no choice but to bring in a new budget. No one expected much. In the days leading up to the speech, the media talked about green initiatives, municipal infrastructure, more aid to students, and minor tinkering with the GST. Yawners all!

So, when Flaherty rose to speak, expectations were low and the public was largely uninterested. He attempted to change that right off the top.

"Mr. Speaker," he intoned in the usual formality of the House of Commons, "the budget is balanced. Taxes have been cut. And Canadians will now have a powerful new incentive to save money, tax-free: the Tax-Free Savings Account that we are announcing today."[1]

Tax-Free Savings Accounts (TFSAs), which no one had previously thought much about, were suddenly centre stage in the most important parliamentary event of the year.

From there, the minister droned on about the strength of the Canadian economy and all the great things the Conservatives had done for taxpayers since taking office in February 2006. He was about one-third of the way through the Budget Speech when he returned to the only major new initiative he had to offer.

"If we are to help families prepare for the long term, we must ensure Canadians have the right incentives to save for the future," he said. "Saving isn't always easy. But it's important. Unfortunately, for too long, government punished people who did the right thing.

"As one of my constituents recently said to me, 'I go to work. I collect my pay. I pay my taxes. And after I pay my expenses each month, I try to put some money away. I don't have a lot. But I am reaching my goal.

"'Yet, the federal government taxes me on what I earn on my savings and my investments. Savings and investments I socked away with after-tax income. Why am I being punished for doing the right thing?'

"Mr. Speaker, he's right. And we're going to change that.

"The Government will unveil the single most important personal savings vehicle since the introduction of the RRSP: the Tax-Free Savings Account. This flexible, registered, general-purpose account will allow Canadians to watch their savings grow, tax-free.

"It's the first account of its kind in Canadian history."

Flaherty offered a few examples of how the new program would benefit ordinary Canadians. It would, he suggested, help young people save for their first car or their first home. It would help seniors "stretch their retirement savings further."

In fact, TFSAs would allow "every Canadian to set aside a bit of cash each month for a special project, to help their kids, or to simply treat themselves."[2]

Best of all, the program would not be a major drain on government revenue, at least initially. In the accompanying Budget Papers, the Department of Finance estimated that

TFSAs would cost Ottawa only $5 million in lost revenue in the 2008–2009 fiscal year—a mere pittance.

The program would gradually become more expensive over time: $50 million in forgone revenue in 2009–2010, rising to $385 million by 2012–2013. But that was still just a drop in the bucket for a government that at the time was collecting more than $240 billion in annual revenue.

Eventually, some 20 years down the road, TFSAs would cost Ottawa an estimated $3 billion annually, Mr. Flaherty estimated. But that would be a problem for some future finance minister to deal with.

First reactions to the new savings plan were tepid for the most part. Media reports tended to focus on the economic aspects of the budget and on the comment by then Liberal leader Stéphane Dion that his party might vote against it and bring down the government. (He quickly backed off that position.)

The *National Post* was one of the few newspapers to highlight the TFSA program, calling it "the major budget surprise." However, the *Post* commented that it was "only one of a grab bag of relatively inexpensive goodies."

Jeff Rubin, who at the time was chief economist of CIBC World Markets, said that making TFSAs the star attraction of the budget was "bizarre." He told the *Post*: "It was really trivial. They are forecasting a $50-million tax expenditure next year for three-and-a-half million taxpayers. It works out to $14 per person … [that] doesn't seem to me to be what the centre piece of a budget should be. You have to have something sexy in there."[3]

(Seven months later, CIBC published a report that predicted TFSAs would generate $20 billion worth of business for Bay Street in 2009 and $115 billion in five years.[4] As of June 2011, Canadians had invested $54.4 billion in Tax-Free Savings Accounts according to data compiled by financial services consulting firm Investor Economics.)

Over at *The Globe and Mail*, writer Steven Chase suggested that Tax-Free Savings Accounts were "the Tories' attempt to make up for the fact they have not delivered on a poorly drafted 2006 election promise for a tax break on capital gains that would have immediately cost Ottawa billions of dollars annually."[5]

Rob Carrick, personal finance columnist for *The Globe and Mail*, was more enthusiastic, writing, "If the government gets this budget passed, TFSAs will become ubiquitous in a few years. Even though the tax savings aren't dramatic, most households will have at least a few of these plans. The TFSA is the sort of measure you rarely see introduced."[6]

Of course, the budget did pass through Parliament, the regulations were put into place, and now TFSAs are part of our investment options. Most Canadians completely forgot about them in the 10 months between announcement and implementation on January 1, 2009. But now they've been around for a few years and more than eight and a half million accounts have been opened. If you don't have a plan, it's time to start reaping the benefits of this unique program.

2
Some History

The idea of the Tax-Free Savings Account did not spring fully formed from the mind of Finance Minister Jim Flaherty. In fact, his predecessors, Liberal Finance Ministers John Manley and Ralph Goodale, had raised the issue in the 2003 and 2004 budgets with a promise that it would be studied.

In the 2003 budget, the government said it would "examine and consult" on whether what were at the time called Tax-Prepaid Savings Plans (TPSPs) might be "a useful and appropriate additional savings vehicle for Canadians."

In Annex 9 of the 2004 Budget Plan, the government gave the impression that the idea was moving up on the priority list. The document stated: "Finance officials consulted with interested groups, experts, and academics on the tax treatment of savings and TPSPs. The discussions were helpful in gathering views on how the tax treatment of savings could be improved and on TPSPs in particular. The Department is reviewing the views brought forward and is continuing to examine and assess TPSPs and other approaches to improve the tax treatment of savings. In the consultation, the question of whether a new type of savings plan such as a TPSP could be appropriate for Canada raised a number of important issues which require further consideration."[1]

But there was no reference to the plan in Goodale's 2005 budget (his final one, as it turned out). At the time, an official with the Department of Finance told me that, after a meeting between senior officials and unnamed experts, it had been decided to shelve the program and simply raise RRSP contribution limits instead.

The reasons for abandoning the concept at that time were never clearly spelled out. However, those familiar with the discussions believe that officials in Finance were concerned about two issues: the cost of such a program over time and the potential political fallout when Guaranteed Income Supplement (GIS) recipients with RRSPs or Registered Retirement Income Funds (RRIFs) caught on to the fact that their benefits were being clawed back as they drew out money while people with TFSAs were not being similarly penalized. As well, there had been growing complaints over the years about the complexity of the tax system, and introducing TFSAs would add another dimension to that problem.

Another factor was the absence of any strong voter constituency to support the idea. The social rationale for the TFSA concept is that it will be of the greatest benefit to people with modest incomes. But they don't have the kind of political clout that, for example, farmers and manufacturers do.

So the TPSP concept remained in limbo for four years, until Jim Flaherty suddenly, and unexpectedly, resurrected it as TFSA in the 2008 budget.

As I noted in Chapter 1, there had been no hint it was coming. Pre-budget speculation took a "cupboard is bare" stance, noting that the finance minister had trotted out all his goodies in the previous fall's Economic Statement, which at the time was expected to kick off an election campaign. However, the opposition parties refused to co-operate with that scheme by defeating the Conservatives in the House of Commons, leaving Flaherty with nothing more to give.

The minister went out of his way to dampen budget expectations, saying in advance that he was not going to "throw money around" or put the country back into deficit by cutting taxes further.

"The fiscal chickens have come home, and are roosting uneasily on Jim Flaherty's shoulders," *The Globe and Mail* commented in a pre-budget editorial. "His options are far narrower now. His leeway is lost. The GST was the wrong tax to cut, at the wrong time. Now Mr. Flaherty has to pinch pennies."[2]

Faced with the prospect of a ho-hum budget in what would likely be an election year (and was, as it turned out), the finance minister and his staff started casting around for ideas. In pre-budget consultations with a range of business people, academics, and special interest groups, Finance officials kept returning to two key themes: demographics and retirement. As a subtext, the minister was very aware of the lingering anger among many seniors over his decision to impose a tax on income trusts, which was announced October 31, 2006, and eventually implemented on January 1, 2011.

In its "shadow budget" brief to the government prior to the 2008 budget, the C.D. Howe Institute returned to the theme of Tax-Free Savings Accounts, which it had been promoting since 2001 (more on that in a moment). However, it rated only six lines in a 13-page report—it was almost as if the institute had given up.[3]

Whether it was that reference or something else that was the trigger, the minister seized on the idea. It was a good ideological fit: The concept had been part of his party's 2004 campaign platform (a campaign the Tories lost to Paul Martin's Liberals). On page 16 of the platform, a one-line sentence in the tax section had made this promise: "Introduce a new Registered Lifetime Savings Plan that will allow Canadians to withdraw their money tax-free."[4]

Interestingly, the concept was not restated in the 2006 platform, Stand Up for Canada. Instead, the Tories promised a much more sweeping overhaul of investment policy, saying they would "eliminate the capital gains tax for individuals on the sale of assets when the proceeds are reinvested within six months." Expanding on this, the platform went on: "Canadians who invest, or inherit cottages or family heirlooms, should be able to sell those assets and plough their profits back into the economy without taking a tax hit. It is time government rewarded Canadians who reinvest their money and create jobs." When I visited the official website of the Conservative Party in September 2008, while the election campaign was on, the 2006 platform had been expunged. A Google search enabled me to retrieve it from www.scribd.com.[5]

The 2004 campaign promise was clearly based on the same concept that Goodale had mused about in the 2003 and 2004 budgets, which is perhaps why the Conservatives chose to abandon it in 2006. But by early winter 2008, things were looking desperate and Flaherty needed a showcase idea that wouldn't cost much but that would have broad appeal and look good in the media headlines. The TFSA concept fit the bill—especially the negligible initial cost. It also had the added attraction of addressing the 2006 capital gains promise, albeit on a much-scaled-back basis. The minister had his officials massage it into a comprehensive plan and took it to Prime Minister Harper, who micromanages everything in Ottawa these days. Once Harper signed on, Cabinet approval was virtually a rubber stamp. Months later, during the 2008 election campaign, Harper described TFSAs as "our first cut" at capital gains tax reform during an interview with Amanda Lang, who was then with the Business News Network and is now with CBC.

So both the Liberals and the Conservatives looked at the TFSA concept between 2003 and 2005, although it was never presented as a high priority. But where did the original idea come from?

The British Model

Britain created a similar program over a decade ago, in April 1999. The Individual Savings Account (ISA) has become quite popular. According to British Government statistics, almost 24 million Britons had ISA accounts at the end of the 2009–2010 fiscal year (the latest statistics available at the time of writing). As of 2011, the total amount invested in ISAs and predecessor plans was almost £385 million.

The Canadian TFSA concept is closely modelled on the British program, but in some ways it offers more flexibility to investors. The British plan gives people two options. One is called a cash ISA, the other a stocks and shares ISA.[6] These must be separate plans and cannot be combined, making them more awkward than a TFSA, which can include all types of securities, depending on the type of plan chosen.

However, the British can sock away a lot more money in ISAs than Canadians can invest in TFSAs. As of 2012, all U.K. residents can invest up to £11,280 annually in their plans. Using an exchange rate of £1 equals CDN$1.60, this means U.K. residents can contribute the equivalent of CDN$18,048 a year to an ISA, more than three times the contribution limit in this country.[7]

The U.K. program was expanded in 2011 with the introduction of individual savings accounts for children, known as "Junior ISAs." Parents can set up these plans for children under 18 and contribute up to £3600 a year to them (about CDN$5700). Like regular ISAs and TFSAs, no tax is payable on any interest, dividends, or capital gains earned in the account. Any money contributed or earned in a Junior ISA belongs to the child (not the parents). At age 18, the child can decide whether to withdraw the funds or keep them in the plan, in which case it would become a regular IRA.

There has been no suggestion that Ottawa will introduce a Junior TFSA in Canada—currently, no one under 18 can open an account. But once the budget is balanced again, a future government might consider the idea.

The Roth IRA

In the United States, the closest thing to the ISA or the TFSA is the Roth Individual Retirement Account (Roth IRA). It actually pre-dates the ISA, having been created in 1998, but it is nowhere near as attractive a savings vehicle as the other two.

As with the British and Canadian plans, contributions to a Roth IRA are not tax-deductible. Unlike the others, however, the maximum annual amount that can be contributed is determined by age and income level. In 2012, Americans under age 50 were allowed to contribute a maximum of $5000 a year, while older citizens could contribute up to $6000. However, high-income earners are not allowed to contribute to these plans. In 2012, the cut-off for a married couple filing a joint return was US$183,000. For a single person, it was US$125,000. The income figures are adjusted annually for inflation.

Profits earned by investments in a Roth IRA are tax-sheltered but can only be withdrawn from the plan tax-free after a holding period of five years or once the investor reaches the age of 59 and six months. None of these constraints applies to Canadian TFSAs.

The Role of the C.D. Howe Institute

The leading advocate for the introduction of Tax-Free Savings Accounts in Canada was the C.D. Howe Institute, a non-partisan think-tank based in Toronto that has been an influential voice in public policy since 1958. (C.D. Howe was a senior Liberal Cabinet minister who served in Parliament for 22 years.)

The institute began advocating what it called Tax-Prepaid Savings Plans (TPSPs) as early as February 2001, in a study titled *A New Option for Retirement Savings: Tax-Prepaid Savings Plans*. Authors Jonathan Kesselman, an economics professor at the University of British Columbia, and Finn Poschmann, now vice-president of research at the C.D. Howe Institute, argued that the existing retirement savings system did not work well for lower-income people and increased the likelihood that they would need support from the public purse in their later years. The document attracted little media interest.

In 2003, the institute raised the ante with the publication of a scathing attack on the unfairness of existing savings plans as they relate to low-income Canadians. The paper was titled *New Poverty Traps: Means Testing and Modest-Income Seniors.*[8] The author, Richard Shillington, holds a doctoral degree in statistics and has been carrying out research into health, social, and economic policies for more than 30 years. His analysis raised serious issues relating to how lower-income seniors who have saved for their retirement are penalized by the way in which government support programs are administered.

Shillington did not mince words. Millions of people who are at or approaching retirement age "are victims of a fraud, however unintentional," he wrote. Saving through RRSPs was likely to make them poorer in retirement, not better off, because most of their RRSP income "will be confiscated by income-tested programs and income taxes."

Government policy-makers were urged to take a close look at the situation and to introduce policies to deal with it as quickly as possible. Specifically, Shillington advocated the creation of TPSPs, similar to the British ISA or the Roth IRA in the United States, which, he said, would meet the retirement savings needs of lower-income Canadians more effectively.

The Liberal government of the day didn't act, so in November 2004, the institute launched yet another initiative. Finn Poschmann and then senior vice-president and director of research (now CEO) William B.P. Robson co-authored another detailed backgrounder on the topic.

Titled *Saving's Grace: A Framework to Promote Financial Independence for Low-Income Canadians*, the report criticized the federal government for creating a range of savings plans for retirement and education that were better suited to the needs of middle- and upper-income people.[9] Plans such as RRSPs and Registered Pension Plans (RPPs) are not useful for lower-income Canadians, they argued, because the tax savings they offer are negligible (RRSP contributions are treated as deductions, which means the higher a person's bracket, the greater the tax savings). When the money is needed, any withdrawals are taxed, perhaps at a higher rate than the value of the original deduction. Plus, any pension or RRIF payments or RRSP withdrawals reduce eligibility for a range of government benefits, such as the Guaranteed Income Supplement, and government tax credits.

The report urged the federal government to create a new, broadly based, easy-to-understand savings program that would be available to all Canadians, regardless of income. The plan should have as few restrictions as possible, offer generous carry-forward provisions, and allow tax-free withdrawals at any time. Especially important, withdrawals should not be considered as income for means-tested programs, subsidies, and tax credits.

The authors concluded by calling the case for such a plan "compelling." In particular, they said that, TPSPs would "let many low-income earners escape the punitive treatment they now suffer at the hands of federal and provincial taxes and benefit claw-backs."

Reading the document today, it seems to have been the blueprint used by the Conservatives for the plan introduced in the 2008 budget, right down to the smallest detail. Not surprisingly, Robson and his colleagues were elated. "It was a worthy centrepiece for a budget," he told me. "This is a revolutionary type of savings vehicle for Canada."

Jim Flaherty acknowledged the role the institute played in bringing TFSAs to reality when he visited its headquarters a few days after his budget was unveiled. A framed, autographed copy of his budget speech now hangs on the wall in Poschmann's office.

The Next Steps

But the story isn't over yet. There are still some challenges to overcome if TFSAs are going to function at maximum efficiency.

Canada has a patchwork quilt of social-assistance programs, with conditions and restrictions that vary greatly from one province to another. William Robson described the net effect as "fiendishly complicated and fantastically uncoordinated."

Unless provincial and territorial laws are changed, social programs that apply means tests and/or asset tests to determine eligibility will discourage lower-income people from using TFSAs to save money.

A brief published on September 30, 2008, by the C.D. Howe Institute said that saving money will be "pointless" for anyone who faces clawbacks of social benefits for doing so.[10]

"Having modest savings (as low as $560 in Ontario for a single welfare recipient) can make one ineligible for support programs, like social assistance, which include asset tests," said the brief's authors, John Stapleton and Richard Shillington. "When governments penalize beneficiaries for saving, by reducing program benefits, these programs become traps."

The brief called on the provinces and territories to pass legislation to ensure that TFSAs work properly. This would be achieved by specifying a level up to which people could accumulate TFSA savings without losing benefits, by defining to whom the ceiling will apply (current recipients, new applicants, or both), and by clarifying the conditions under which people can make TFSA withdrawals without jeopardizing social benefits.

The institute also recommended that governments consider building on the TFSA platform by supplementing the savings of lower-income people. The Canada Education Savings Grant, which is added to Registered Education

Savings Plan (RESP) contributions, was cited as an example. Unfortunately, as of fall 2012, Finn Poschmann, vice-president of research at the C.D. Howe Institute, said that the provinces as a group have made very little progress on this.

Another area where the institute believes governments are off base is in Ottawa's approach to Pooled Registered Pension Plans (PRPPs). The Conservative government has touted these as the answer to Canada's growing pension crisis but an analysis published by the institute in the summer of 2012 says they fall well short of that. Authors James Pierlot and Alex Laurin say that, unless a TFSA-style option is offered within the PRPP framework, "lower- and middle-income workers over a lifetime will be much better off financially to save for retirement in TFSAs."

As an example, they looked at the case of a 30-year-old single individual in Alberta with employment earnings of $50,000, rising at 2.5 percent per year for the next 35 years, who saved an average of 6.7 percent a year. They concluded this person would enjoy 26 percent more consumable annuity income after retirement by using a TFSA instead of a PRPP or an RRSP.

This is not an isolated case, they stressed. "For low-income individuals, tax-prepaid savings such as TFSAs are preferable by a large margin," they wrote. Their advice—amend the legislation to permit the use of Tax-Free Pension Accounts (TFPA) and allow PRPP members to contribute to them.

"Analogous to a TFSA, which allows tax-free accumulations and withdrawals, a TFPA should be available to all members but designed primarily for the needs of low- to mid-income workers," they conclude.[11]

So there may be more chapters to come in the TFSA story. But everyone seems to agree that what we now have in place is a valuable first step.

3
The Basic Rules

Once people understand the concept of TFSAs, they quickly embrace the idea. A Scotiabank survey carried out a few months after the 2008 budget announcement found that although awareness was still low at the time, Canadians reacted enthusiastically when the key points of the program were explained.

"Most Canadians single out the tax savings as most appealing, although many also find the flexibility to withdraw funds without compromising contribution room compelling," the survey analysis concluded. "Overall, most Canadians (60 percent) view the TFSA as an 'ideal savings and investment account' for them."[1]

As it turned out, the Scotiabank findings were accurate. Canadians began opening accounts even before the official launch date after several financial institutions started aggressively promoting the plans in the fall of 2008. Less than two months after ING DIRECT Canada began offering TFSAs in October of that year, the president of the company, Peter Aceto, reported that 170,000 accounts had been opened. "We've actually been a bit surprised by the overwhelming response," he said.

Despite the initial enthusiasm, it soon became apparent

that many people had little understanding of the rules governing TFSAs. And based on more recent surveys, that is still the case.

For example, in early 2012 ING DIRECT released the results of a poll conducted the previous fall by Angus Reid. It came up with some startling conclusions. More than one-third of the 1668 people surveyed (37 percent) said they had only a vague idea of what a TFSA is. Another 14 percent said they didn't understand how the plans work while 13 percent replied that they had never heard of TFSAs. Considering that the plans had been available for three years at that point, those results were disappointing.

ING president Peter Aceto commented: "The Tax-Free Savings Account is an invaluable tool when it comes to saving money for the future but unfortunately many Canadians are unclear about the rules which can lead to overcontribution mistakes and frustration for savers. Like any registered product there are certain rules when it comes to investing in a TFSA, but it takes minimal effort to familiarize yourself with the ins and outs of the account."

Mr. Aceto is absolutely right. You need to know the rules before you invest one penny in a TFSA, otherwise you could end up making some expensive mistakes. So, before we get into the strategies for making TFSAs work most effectively for you, let's review the key points you need to know about these plans and how they differ from RRSPs and RESPs.

Age limit. In theory, anyone 18 or older can open a TFSA. That's what the federal legislation says. However, sometimes things are not always simple in Canada because of conflicting federal and provincial jurisdictions. This is one of those cases.

In some provinces and territories, the age of majority is 19 (British Columbia, New Brunswick, Newfoundland and Labrador, Northwest Territories, Nova Scotia, Nunavut, and Yukon). This means that contracts entered into by 18-year-olds, who are legally minors in those jurisdictions, can be voided by the courts if challenged.

As a result, Ottawa amended its rules in 2009 so that 18-year-olds in those provinces will not be allowed to open a TFSA until they turn 19. However, the accumulation of contribution room will start at 18 even if a plan cannot be opened for another year.

There is no maximum age for holding a TFSA. This differs in two important ways from RRSPs. Although most people don't realize it, even a child can open an RRSP as long as he or she has earned income. If your baby girl is chosen to star in a television commercial, the income she earns could be used to open an RRSP. That's not the case with TFSAs—only adults need apply.

At the other end of the age scale, the government does not allow you to hold an RRSP past December 31 of the year in which you turn 71. At that time, you must cash in the plan, convert it to a RRIF, or buy an annuity. That left older Canadians without a simple and cheap tax shelter and, as the population ages, more people were becoming concerned about that.

TFSAs are the answer. Since there is no termination date

for these plans, you can keep contributing to them (thereby sheltering investment income) until the day you die.

Carry-forwards. The rules are similar to those for RRSPs in that any unused contribution room may be carried forward indefinitely. You do not have to file a tax return to accumulate carry-forward room. However, if you don't do so, the Canada Revenue Agency will not be able to keep track of the amount you are allowed to put into a TFSA. You will need to do that yourself.

Anyone who was at least 18 years old when TFSAs were launched in 2009 and who has never contributed to a plan now has $20,000 in accumulated contribution room available ($5000 for each year from 2009 to 2012). Add the 2013 limit, expected to be $5500, and the total amount that can be put into a new plan is $25,500.

Contribution limit. The initial contribution limit was set at $5000 per person and that maximum applied through 2012. The limit is indexed to inflation and, theoretically at least, adjusted annually. But there is some small print in the regulations that prevented any change in the maximum for several years. It is expected to rise to $5500 in 2013 (no official announcement had been made at the time of this revision). But after that increase, it will probably be a long time before we see another one.

Here's why. The Department of Finance decided to move away from the standard annual indexing formula that is used for tax brackets, CPP payments, tax credits, and so forth. Instead, Finance introduced a new type of indexing, which, it says, provides "simplification and certainty." (It will also slow the drain that TFSAs will have on the public purse, but Finance officials say that was not a major factor in the decision.) The TFSA formula requires that indexing be done in increments of $500. This means the limit will be rounded up or down each year. The effect was to delay the first increase in the TFSA contribution limit until the inflation factor reached at least $250.

At an annual inflation rate of 2 percent, that would have happened in the 2012 tax year. But inflation in this country has been unusually low in the wake of the 2008–2009 stock market crash and the resulting economic slowdown. As a result, the indexing calculation came up seven dollars short at $5243, so the 2012 limit stayed at $5000.

As of mid-2012, inflation in Canada was running at 1.5 percent on an annualized basis. If that level held for the rest of the year, the TFSA index would move up to $5322, which would be more than enough to move the contribution level to $5500.

But don't expect another increase any time soon. Assuming an average annual inflation rate of 2 percent and using $5322 in 2013 as a starting point, the following chart indicates what we can expect in changes to the maximum contribution limit in the next few years.

Year	Cumulative inflation factor*	Contribution limit
2014	$5428	$5500
2015	$5537	$5500
2016	$5648	$5500
2017	$5760	$6000
2018	$5876	$6000
2019	$5993	$6000
2020	$6113	$6000
2021	$6236	$6000
2022	$6360	$6500

*Assumes annual inflation rate of 2 percent.

As you can see, the next increase in the annual maximum contribution, to $6000, will not occur until 2017 unless inflation runs at a higher rate than the Bank of Canada target. It will be 2022 before the limit moves up again, to $6500. Of course, if inflation averages less than 2 percent, any increases will be delayed for a year or more.

To put this into perspective, the maximum allowable RRSP contribution for high-income earners in 2013 is $23,820. It will take decades for TFSAs to come anywhere near that. This will become an important consideration when we examine TFSAs versus RRSPs as retirement savings options in Chapter 6.

There is a possibility that the TFSA limit could move higher sooner than projected. During the 2011 election campaign, Prime Minister Stephen Harper promised to double the contribution limit once the federal budget is brought back into balance, which at the time was projected to happen in 2015. But that's still a long way off and campaign promises made years before have a way of being forgotten. So don't hold your breath.

Contributions in kind. You don't need to have cash to make a TFSA contribution. You can also build a plan through what are known as contributions in kind. This allows you to deposit securities you already own directly to a TFSA. For example, suppose you have $4500 invested in a guaranteed investment certificate (GIC) that does not mature for three years. You can start tax-sheltering the interest immediately by contributing to your plan. You have to pay tax on the interest you earn up to the time you contributed it to your TFSA, but after that, all your profit is tax-free. However, there is a potential trap here. If the total value of the GIC (principal plus accrued interest) exceeds your current contribution limit, you run the risk of an overcontribution. Before you issue instructions, check the current value of the certificate and make sure you have enough contribution room to accommodate it.

The rules governing TFSA contributions in kind are the same as those for RRSPs, so there are a couple of points you need to consider before making use of this strategy.

First, if you make a contribution in kind, the Canada Revenue Agency treats the transaction as if you sold the security on the day it went into the plan. This means that if you have a capital gain, for example on a stock or mutual fund, that gain is triggered when you make the contribution and must be declared on your income tax return for that year.

The second point to remember is that, while you will

have to pay tax on any capital gains created by contributing a security to a TFSA, you may not claim a capital loss. This distortion in the tax rules has burned some people who decided to dump losing stocks into their RRSPs only to discover too late that the loss was not tax-deductible. So never contribute a money-losing security directly to a TFSA. Sell it first, thereby creating a deductible capital loss, and then put the cash from the sale into the plan.

Death. When you die, the assets in your TFSA can be transferred to the plan of your spouse or common-law partner if he or she is named as your successor holder in the TFSA contract and/or your will. Things get more complicated when the last spouse or partner dies, but essentially all of the assets in a TFSA at the time of death can pass to the next generation tax-free. More details are presented in Chapter 10.

Deposit insurance. Certain types of TFSA deposits are covered up to $100,000 by the Canada Deposit Insurance Corporation (CDIC), including cash, term deposits, and guaranteed investment certificates. But as a general rule, most securities, including stocks and mutual funds, are not covered. That includes money market funds. For complete details on federal deposit insurance, visit www.cdic.ca.

Eligibility. You must be a resident of Canada to open a TFSA. You have to provide your Social Insurance Number (SIN) and date of birth when you set up a plan.

Foreign funds. You can contribute foreign funds, such as U.S. dollars, to a TFSA. However, the plan administrator is required by law to convert the funds to Canadian dollars, using the date of the transaction, when reporting this information to the CRA. The total amount of your contribution, in Canadian dollars, cannot exceed your TFSA contribution room.

Income splitting. The usual income-attribution rules do not apply to TFSAs. This means one spouse can provide the money for the other to open an account without penalty. So, even if the other spouse has no income or savings, he or she can have a TFSA. Over the years, this could lead to big tax savings for families. See Chapter 9 for more information.

Income testing. TFSA withdrawals are not considered as income. So they don't compromise your eligibility for income-tested tax credits such as the Age Credit, the Canada Child Tax Benefit, the Working Income Tax Benefit, or the GST credit. You can withdraw money from TFSAs without affecting Employment Insurance benefits. For older Canadians, TFSA withdrawals don't affect their eligibility for programs such as the Guaranteed Income Supplement (GIS) and don't result in Old Age Security (OAS) clawbacks.

This is very important for lower-income seniors. Under current rules, GIS payments are cut by 50 cents for every $1 worth of income a recipient receives over $3500 a year. This includes the income from RRSP withdrawals and RRIF payments, so low-income seniors receiving GIS see their payments eroded because they made the effort to save a little for retirement. That's why, in the 2003 paper Dr. Richard Shillington prepared for the C.D. Howe Institute, he suggested that people who expect to qualify for GIS should not make RRSP contributions and advised the government to introduce a TFSA-like program instead.[2] It took six years, but it finally happened.

Interest deductibility. You may borrow money to invest in a TFSA, but you cannot claim the interest on the loan as a tax deduction. These rules are the same as for RRSPs.

(In their booklet on Tax-Free Savings Accounts, the Tax and Estate Planning team at Mackenzie Financial suggests that you can make the interest deductible by transferring assets from a non-registered portfolio to a TFSA. "Your non-registered assets could then be repurchased with borrowed funds," the team says. "In this case, a direct link from the borrowed money to an eligible non-registered investment would be established, and interest should be tax-deductible."[3])

Investments. TFSAs are highly flexible when it comes to the investments you can choose. The rules for qualified securities are the same as those applied to RRSPs. Almost anything is allowed: guaranteed investment certificates, mutual funds, stocks (Canadian and foreign), bonds, gold, and cash. Even shares in a small business are eligible under certain conditions (see Chapter 12 for more details). The major exceptions (as with RRSPs) are real estate and non-arm's-length investments. If you are uncertain whether an investment qualifies, get professional advice before going ahead, because the penalties for including non-eligible investments in a TFSA can be severe. In October 2009, the Department of Finance announced amendments to the Income Tax Act that impose a 100-percent tax on any income attributed to non-qualified investments held in a TFSA.

Loan collateral. Unlike RRSPs, a TFSA can be used as collateral for loans. This could be useful in a situation where you suddenly need cash to deal with an emergency but the money in your TFSA is not accessible, perhaps because it has been invested in a locked-in GIC. If the lender is satisfied that the assets in the plan are sound, the TFSA can serve as collateral for a cash advance.

There is one important exception. In order to prevent TFSA contribution room from being "sold" or "rented," any loan agreement must be on an arm's-length basis. If the propriety of a loan is questioned, you'll have to be able to show that the loan was not intended to "enable another person or partnership to benefit from the exemption from tax" provided by the TFSA exemption.

Living abroad. If you leave Canada after opening a TFSA, you can maintain the account and continue to make withdrawals. However, you will have to check whether such withdrawals would be regarded as tax-free by the country in which you are residing. You may not make any new contributions while you are out of the country and no new contribution room will accrue. If you contribute to a TFSA while you are a non-resident, you will be assessed a penalty tax of 1 percent a month until the amount is withdrawn or you become a legal resident again.

(Note: It is possible to be a Canadian resident even if you live outside the country, as long as you have close ties with Canada. This might include having a home and personal property in the country, a spouse or dependents in Canada, being eligible for provincial medical insurance, and so on. More details can be found in the Canada Revenue Agency's Interpretation Bulletin IT-221R.)

Marriage breakdown. TFSA assets can be transferred from the plan of one spouse or partner to the plan of the other in the event of a marriage breakdown. However, in this case, the person from whom the money is transferred is not given new contribution room to compensate, as this is not considered to be a withdrawal. Any such transfer does not count against the contribution room of the spouse or partner who receives the money.

Number of plans. The ING poll found that 27 percent of respondents believed they are only allowed to have one TFSA. That's not the case. As with RRSPs, there is no limit on the number of TFSAs you can open. But common sense suggests that you limit yourself to one plan for ease of administration. If you decide to open a second TFSA, make sure you have a good reason for doing so.

Overcontributions. Avoid making any overcontributions. The penalties are draconian. In October 2009, the Finance

Department announced that any profits from intentional overcontributions will be taxed at a rate of 100 percent! If you make an overcontribution by mistake, withdraw the money from the plan as soon as you discover the error. Unlike with RRSPs, there is no $2000 lifetime overcontribution allowed.

Plan termination. A TFSA ceases to exist when the last account holder dies, the plan ceases to qualify for whatever reason, or the account is not being administered according to the law.

Reporting. Although TFSAs aren't taxable, the Canada Revenue Agency will need to keep tabs on your plan in order to determine how much you are allowed to contribute in any given year. The reporting responsibility is in the hands of the financial institution that administers your plan, which files an annual information return. This includes details of all contributions, withdrawals, and transfers made during the year as well as the value of the plan's assets at the beginning and end of the year.

Originally, the Canada Revenue Agency was supposed to advise taxpayers of the amount they could contribute to their TFSA on the annual notice of assessment. However, that has changed. To find out how much room you have available you have to call CRA Enquiries at 1-800-267-6999 or check your account on the CRA website at www.cra.gc.ca/myaccount.

Spousal plans. Unlike RRSPs, there are no spousal TFSAs. Also, there is no such thing as a joint TFSA—each plan is the property of one individual. However, one spouse is permitted to give the other the money to open a TFSA. See the earlier section on income splitting for more details.

Swaps. Swaps involve exchanging cash or securities from outside a TFSA for assets of equal value inside the plan. For example, you may wish to put $5000 worth of new cash into your TFSA and withdraw $5000 worth of mutual fund units simultaneously. Initially, the Department of Finance said swaps would not be allowed because the assets coming out of the plan would represent a withdrawal and therefore would not create new contribution room until the following year.

Then, in January 2009, the Canada Revenue Agency adopted a more liberal stance, saying TFSA swaps would be treated in the same way as RRSP swaps. The CRA has responsibility for interpreting the tax laws, so as a result of its position, TFSA swaps were legal—but only for a short time.

In October 2009, after receiving evidence that some people were aggressively using swaps to dramatically increase the value of their TFSAs, Finance announced changes to the Income Tax Act that prohibited such transactions from either non-registered or registered accounts (such as RRSPs). So swaps are once again off limits and will attract hefty penalties. Don't try to do them.

Tax deductions. There are none. You do not receive any tax relief for a TFSA contribution. Any money that goes into a plan is on an after-tax basis (RESPs operate the same way). This is a major difference between TFSAs and RRSPs—one that will certainly cause a lot of head-scratching as people decide which plan they should contribute to.

Taxes. Although you don't get a tax deduction when you contribute, all withdrawals from your TFSA are tax-free. The investment income earned within the plan is fully sheltered, forever—unlike RRSPs, where all investment income earned within a plan is taxed at your marginal taxation rate when you withdraw it. TFSAs thus provide a way to earn investment income without incurring any tax liability, now or in the future.

TFSA year-end. For purposes of contributions and carry-forwards, TFSAs operate on a calendar-year basis, so the annual cut-off date is December 31. This means TFSAs use the same clock as RESPs. (RRSP contributions, by contrast, may be made up to 60 days after the end of the calendar year.)

Transfers. You can transfer assets from one of your own TFSAs to another one. This is called a "qualifying transfer." If you want to move the money into an RRSP, you can make a tax-free withdrawal from the TFSA and contribute directly to the RRSP, which will generate a tax deduction. However, and this question has been asked of me a lot, you cannot transfer money from an RRSP to a TFSA. Many people thought that would be a great idea because it would avoid the tax on RRSP withdrawals. Sadly, it's a non-starter.

Withdrawals. You can take money out of a TFSA at any time, with no tax consequences. You don't even have to declare it on your income tax return—it is like withdrawing money from your bank savings account. And here is an interesting twist: Unlike with RRSPs, any amount you withdraw is added back to your contribution limit for the next year. (Exceptions include withdrawals relating to overcontributions, prohibited or non-qualifying investments, asset transfers, and any profits derived from these sources.)

Let's suppose you accumulate $20,000 in a TFSA between now and 2015. At that point, you decide to draw out $15,000 to help pay for a new car. Assuming that the annual contribution limit at that time is $5500, your personal limit for 2016 will be $20,500—the basic maximum plus the amount you took out of the plan for the car purchase.

Note that you cannot recontribute withdrawn amounts within the same calendar year. You must wait until January 1 of the year following. So if you withdraw $2000 in 2013, that amount does not become part of your legal contribution room until 2014.

4

The "Magic" of TFSAs

Quick now, what is often referred to as the "eighth wonder of the world"?

The answer is compound interest. It's a simple but powerful way to get rich, provided you have time and a little self-discipline.

Before we go any further, let me clarify an important point. Although the term generally used is compound interest, what we are really talking about is compounded *profits* from investment income of any kind. That can include dividends, fund distributions, rental income, capital gains, and anything else you earn from your invested money. So for the purposes of this discussion, I'll use the all-encompassing term of compound income.

Compound income simply amounts to profit earning more profit. If you invest $1 at 4 percent, after one year you'll have $1.04. Now you'll start to earn income on that extra four cents as well as on your original dollar. It doesn't happen quickly, but over the years, that can add up to a lot of money.

The Rule of 72 is a classic way to calculate how long it will take for an amount of money to double in value through compounding. To use it, simply divide 72 by the return on the invested money. For instance, if you invest $1000 at an annual rate of return of 4 percent, it will take 18 years for your money to double (72 ÷ 4). But if your money earns 6 percent, it will double in only 12 years (72 ÷ 6).

Of course, this assumes that you get to keep all the investment income for yourself. In reality, the government keeps dipping its sticky fingers into your profits. And that's been the big problem for Canadians until now. We've had no way to fully benefit from the magic of compound income in this country because Ottawa and the provinces are always taking a share of the pie.

You may ask, what about RRSPs? While it's true that any investment income that is earned in retirement savings plans is tax-sheltered, you're hit with a big tax bite when you take the money out.

For example, suppose you contribute $1000 a year to an RRSP over 30 years and invest the money in guaranteed investment certificates that pay an average annual return of 5 percent (recent rates have been much lower but this is only an illustration). At the end of that time, the plan is valued at $69,761. Subtracting your $30,000 in contributions, you have earned investment income totalling almost $40,000.

But as soon as you start taking money out of that RRSP, the government swoops in and taxes it. If you are in the 30-percent bracket, you'll give back $12,000 of the income you've earned over all those years to the tax folks. You get to keep only $28,000 for yourself. The 5 percent you thought you earned ended up only being about 4 percent in after-tax terms. Plus you will also pay tax at the 30-percent rate on your contributions as they come out, adding another $9000 to the tax bill.

If you are in a 40-percent bracket, your after-tax gain on the $40,000 profit you earned from the GICs drops to $24,000. Suddenly, compounding doesn't seem quite so magical any more.

Tax-Free Savings Accounts change everything. For the first time, we have access to an investment vehicle that allows us to obtain the full benefit of compounding. The income we earn in a TFSA is 100 percent ours to keep. No part of it will be taxed away.

Here's a table that illustrates what this means in terms of wealth building over time and shows the value of the TFSA at the end of various time frames. I've assumed an average annual compound rate of return of 5 percent in all cases.

TFSA Growth at 5 Percent

Annual contribution	10 years	20 years	30 years	40 years
$1000	$13,207	$34,719	$69,761	$126,840
$2000	$26,414	$69,439	$139,522	$253,680
$3000	$39,620	$104,158	$209,282	$380,519
$4000	$52,827	$138,877	$279,043	$507,359
$5000	$66,034	$173,596	$348,804	$634,199

Assumption: Contribution is made at start of year.

In case you're wondering, it would take 50 years for the value of the plan to surpass $1 million based on an annual contribution of $5000. With life expectancy increasing, readers who are 25 today have a realistic hope of achieving that $1 million. Also, remember that couples can save twice as much. We'll examine the implications of that in Chapter 12.

Take a close look at the numbers in this table. There are two key points to take away.

First, start young. Compounding is like a rolling snowball. It takes time to gather speed and mass. The more years a plan has to grow, the more impressive the returns will be.

Look at the $1000 line in the table. After one decade, the plan has only added $3207 to your original $10,000 in contributions. But after 20 years, the investment income earned within the plan has ballooned to $14,719 ($34,719 minus $20,000 in contributions). After 40 years, the magic of compounding has given you a total, tax-free profit of $86,840!

So, the sooner you begin, the more effectively a TFSA can work for you. Obviously, none of us can turn back time. But however old you are today, the same basic rule applies: The sooner you begin, the more effective a TFSA will be.

Second, contribute as much as you can. Slide your eyes down each column. You'll see that the more money you contribute annually, the more profitable a TFSA becomes over the years. If you double the annual contribution from $1000 to $2000, your profit from compounding also doubles after the first decade, from $3207 to $6414. If you are able to contribute the initial maximum amount of $5000 annually, your 10-year profit increases to $16,034. (Of course, these figures assume no withdrawals are made along the way.)

The powerhouse effect of combining high contributions

with many years of growth is apparent in the cell on the bottom right of the table. This shows you how much money is in a plan after 40 years of growth at 5 percent with an annual contribution of $5000. The total is $634,199, which means your tax-free profit after deducting all contributions is $434,199. That's a nice nest egg to draw on in retirement!

An Extra Point of Return

Now let's play with these numbers a little. The next table shows you the value of a TFSA if you are able to add one percentage point of annual return over the years, moving from 5 percent to 6 percent.

TFSA Growth at 6 Percent

Annual contribution	10 years	20 years	30 years	40 years
$1000	$13,972	$38,993	$83,802	$164,048
$2000	$27,943	$77,985	$167,603	$328,095
$3000	$41,915	$116,978	$251,405	$492,143
$4000	$55,887	$155,971	$335,207	$656,191
$5000	$69,858	$194,964	$419,008	$820,238

Assumption: Contribution is made at start of year.

What a difference a percentage point makes over time! After a decade, that extra return doesn't translate into a large profit gain—at the $1000 annual contribution level, the additional growth is only $765, which suggests that for older people the added risk involved may not be worth it.

But look what happens as the years pass and the magic of compounding takes hold. Staying with the $1000 contributor, at the end of the second decade the additional gain is $4274. After 40 years, this person is ahead by $37,208 because he or she invested the money wisely and earned one percentage point more.

Here again, the more you contribute, the greater the impact of the extra percentage point of return. An annual contribution of $5000 that is invested to earn an average annual gain of 5 percent grows to $634,199 after 40 years. But at 6 percent, the TFSA is worth $820,238 at that stage. The extra percentage point has given you an additional $186,039 to help fund your retirement. Now that's impressive!

End-of-Year Contributions

Finally, let's look at one more set of numbers. The tables we've looked at so far assume that TFSA contributions are made at the start of each calendar year, on January 1. Most people, however, tend to put things off. So let's see what happens if the contributions are delayed to the last minute, to December 31 of the same year. Here's what our 6-percent table would look like in those circumstances.

TFSA Growth at 6 Percent

Annual contribution	10 years	20 years	30 years	40 years
$1000	$13,181	$36,786	$79,058	$154,762
$2000	$26,362	$73,571	$158,116	$309,524
$3000	$39,542	$110,357	$237,175	$464,286
$4000	$52,723	$147,142	$316,233	$619,048
$5000	$65,904	$183,928	$395,291	$773,804

Assumption: Contribution is made at end of year.

This may be difficult to believe, but waiting until the end of each year to make a TFSA contribution can end up costing you tens of thousands of dollars in lost profit (the same applies to RRSPs, by the way). Again, you don't notice much of an impact in the early years, but as the compounding snowball begins to gain momentum, the price of delaying starts to add up.

The person who contributes $3000 annually on December 31 of each year has $6621 less profit after 20 years than someone who makes the same contribution 12 months earlier, on January 1.

As we move out to 40 years, the impact of delaying a contribution really hits hard. Someone who puts $5000 a year into a TFSA on January 1 of each year over that time will have a plan worth $820,238. The person who waits until year-end will have only $773,804. That's a difference of more than $46,000, proving once again that procrastination can be expensive.

ACTION SUMMARY

1. Start immediately. Set up a TFSA as soon as you can.
   The more years your money can grow tax-sheltered, the
   wealthier you will be.
2. Contribute as much as possible. Any amount is better than
   nothing, but if you stretch a little, the reward at the end will
   be much greater.
3. Contribute early. Don't wait until New Year's Eve to make
   your annual contribution. Get the money into the plan as
   early in the year as possible.
4. Within reason, aim for a higher return. Don't take
   needless risks with your TFSA money, but don't be overly
   conservative either, especially if you are under 50. An extra
   percentage point of profit will add thousands of dollars to
   your wealth over the years.

5
Rainy Day TFSAs

Every financial expert will tell you the same thing: All families should have an emergency cash reserve to help them get through difficult times. The problem is that in recent years few people have been paying attention to this basic rule of money management. The idea of putting something aside for a rainy day didn't resonate when the sun was shining all the time. However, the deep recession of 2008–2009 made saving for the future a higher priority for many families.

Although it took an economic crisis to force a change in attitude, the long-term result could be positive. In the United States, the savings rate had fallen to close to zero and was threatening to slip into negative territory, a phenomenon unheard of since the Great Depression of the 1930s. In the months following the stock market crash, the U.S. savings rate jumped to 6.2 percent during the April–June period of 2009. It tailed off again as income growth stagnated but was still at 3.6 percent in the first quarter of 2012. That was much better than the Canadian rate for the same period which was only 2.9 percent according to Statistics Canada.[1]

The sub-prime mortgage disaster in the United States was a chilling lesson in just how destructive too much debt can be. Americans lost their homes to foreclosures at a higher rate than at any time since the 1930s. Thousands of decent people ended up on the street because they could not meet their mortgage payments. Had they put some money into an emergency savings account over the years, they might have been able to survive.

Unfortunately, the debt load continues to increase among Canadians. On a national basis, the average household debt-to-income ratio hit a record 152 percent in the first quarter of 2012.

We need to see more emphasis on saving in the next few years or Canadians face an increasing risk of over-extending themselves. Tax-Free Savings Accounts make saving easier and more financially attractive.

Until now, there has not been any truly effective way to build an emergency fund. Putting the money in a regular bank savings account is easy and safe, but it pays no return to speak of. In fact, when inflation and taxes are factored in, your emergency fund probably loses some value each year.

A high-interest savings account is a better choice but, unless it is inside a TFSA, the return on your savings will still be negligible after taxes and inflation are calculated. For example, suppose you put $1000 of emergency money into a high-interest savings account that pays 3 percent a year. You are in the 30-percent tax bracket, and the inflation rate is 2 percent. Your statement shows that you earn $30 a year on your money. But the government grabs $9 of that in taxes, and inflation reduces the buying power of your savings by $20, to $980. Your real return on your savings for that year is only $1! That works out to 0.1 percent. "Why bother?" you may ask.

Some people have tried to get around this dilemma by using their RRSPs as an emergency fund. The RRSP strategy offers the advantage of an immediate tax refund and postpones the tax bite on investment income until the money is withdrawn. But the downside is that this approach could actually end up costing you more in the end. That's because you may have to withdraw cash for an emergency at a time when you are in a higher tax bracket than you were when you originally contributed the money. Also, a withholding tax of anywhere from 10 percent to 30 percent applies to all RRSP withdrawals except in Quebec, where the minimum is 21 percent and the maximum 35 percent. Although you'll get credit for any tax withheld when you file your annual tax return, it means you won't have access to all your money at a time when you may need it most.

The ideal emergency fund allows you quick access to your cash whenever you need it while providing tax-sheltering for the income your money earns in the meantime. That's the precise description of a TFSA. These plans are the perfect vehicles for building your emergency savings account, which means that every family should have one.

If you already have an emergency fund, your first step should be to open a TFSA (and one for your spouse or partner as well) and move the money into the plan to the extent you have available contribution room. If you have not created such a fund, now is the ideal time to start. It should be the first priority in building your TFSA.

Gillian Riley, Scotiabank's senior vice-president, Canadian commercial banking, put it this way: "When thinking about the TFSA and how Canadians can apply it to their personal financial situation, I would recommend that they look at how they use their traditional savings account and consider using the TFSA instead to earn tax-free growth. The TFSA is a tool that should inspire Canadians to save because of its added benefits and versatility."

Of course, the best time to build an emergency fund is when your budget is under control and you can free up some cash. The problem is that people always find something on which to spend any extra money they earn. When budgets are stretched, saving becomes even harder. Sure, an emergency fund may be a fine idea. But after paying the household bills, the mortgage, the car loan, the dentist, and all the other bills, there's nothing left over.

So you must make building your emergency fund a priority. You have to decide that this is a financial cushion your family simply must have and that one way or another you're going to make it happen, even if it means some sacrifices. That's why it needs to be included as an integral part of the family budget. Commitment is half the battle.

How Big a Fund?

Generally, I recommend your emergency fund be equal to at least three months' worth of family take-home pay (after tax). Some experts counsel having a six-month reserve, and I have recently seen some popular U.S. financial gurus suggesting that eight months' worth of income be set aside.

To put this in dollar terms, let's look at the case of a

childless couple, with each person earning taxable income of $60,000. So the total family taxable income is $120,000 a year. The after-tax amount will vary depending on the value of the tax credits the couple has available to them and where they live, due to different provincial rates across the country. An Ontario couple with only basic personal tax credits will have after-tax combined income of about $96,000, based on 2012 tax rates. If we use the three-month formula, they should have at least $24,000 in their emergency fund.

In contrast, a single person living in Nova Scotia who has a taxable income of only $35,000 a year and an after-tax income of $28,709 would need a minimum emergency reserve of about $7200.

These examples illustrate that there is no "right" amount for everyone. Much depends on your personal situation. Income is not the only factor to consider; you must also take into account your financial risk level. A single-income family whose breadwinner is an autoworker in Ontario should try to put more money aside than a couple in Alberta who both work in the public sector, because the risk of job loss is much higher in the automotive industry and the family does not have a second income to fall back on. A family whose main wage earner has a history of illness should have a larger emergency fund than one in which the primary earner is healthy. Families with children need to have more money in reserve than those who are childless.

Putting some cash aside each month for an emergency fund may seem daunting when you're planning a budget. But if you actually have to draw on the fund at some point, you will be thankful you made the effort. So where do you find the money?

I said earlier that commitment is half the battle when it comes to creating an emergency fund. The other half is execution. One way to achieve this goal is to set up a pre-authorized savings plan at your financial institution. Tell them to put aside 3 percent to 5 percent of your income each month (whatever you decide is appropriate) and deposit it into your TFSA. Even if the amount is small, I urge you to start the process. Then add to your savings every time a family member gets a salary increase or you receive some windfall money, such as a tax refund.

Since everyone is allowed to set up a TFSA, a couple could put as much as $11,000 into their plans each year, assuming a contribution rate of $5500 per person. That is a good start toward an emergency fund; for a family with a low financial risk, it might even be enough.

Investment Options

Once you've started saving for an emergency fund, the question is where to invest the cash. There are two priorities to take into account. The first is safety: This is your "rainy day" money, so you don't want to put it at risk. The stock market meltdown that we experienced in the fall/winter of 2008–2009 was a painful reminder of the dangers of aggressive investing.

Your second priority is accessibility. Unless the money is

available to you immediately, you don't have a true emergency fund.

This means you should not invest in any type of locked-in security, such as a non-redeemable guaranteed investment certificate. Such GICs are safe (they are covered by deposit insurance up to the legal limit as long as the maturity date is less than five years) and they offer more attractive interest rates than savings accounts. But they will tie up your money for anywhere up to 10 years, depending on the maturity date (one-year to five-year terms are the most common). That makes them non-starters for emergency funds.

Redeemable GICs are a better choice in that you can get your money out before maturity if needed. However, you may pay an interest rate penalty if you make an early withdrawal, which may inhibit you from using the money even when it is badly needed.

Some financial institutions offer one-year cashable GICs that can be redeemed at any time without penalty. This makes them the most suitable type of GIC for an emergency fund, but there is one big drawback—the interest rate offered may be even less than that paid by a high-interest savings account.

A high-interest account is certainly a decent option for your emergency fund. Even during a period of low interest rates, the returns from these accounts will be higher than those offered by conventional savings accounts. You won't get rich with them but your money will be safe, you'll be able to withdraw it at any time, and the interest you earn will be tax-free. These accounts are especially good choices when interest rates are moving higher, since their rates are adjusted frequently.

If you decide this is the route you want to go, be sure to open your TFSA at a financial institution with a high-interest account that does not have a prohibitive minimum requirement. Check the rates being offered by various companies. For example, in summer 2012, Royal Bank was paying 1.2 percent on its RBC High Interest eSavings Account while President's Choice Financial was offering 1.4 percent on its Tax-Free Income Plus Savings Account. Some people will forgo the extra interest for the convenience of dealing with their current bank. But look at it this way: The President's Choice account was actually paying 16.7 percent more than the RBC account at that point. That's a significant differential! So do some comparison shopping before you make a commitment (rates change frequently). And make sure your account is covered by deposit insurance.

Money Market Funds

Sometimes a money market fund (MMF) may offer a slightly better return than a high-interest savings account, although that has not been the case in recent years. With interest rates so low, MMFs have struggled. The average Canadian fund returned only 0.3 percent over the year to June 30, 2012, and the three-year average annual compound rate of return was almost the same at 0.29 percent.

MMFs invest in short-term securities with an average term to maturity of less than 90 days (although they may hold notes with maturities out to one year). To qualify as a Canadian money market fund, at least 95 percent of the assets must be invested in Canadian-dollar securities.

MMFs have long been considered to be almost risk-free. However, nothing should be taken for granted these days. Even theoretically safe short-term notes can lose some or all of their value, and MMFs are not protected by deposit insurance. In 2007, National Bank had to put up $2 billion to bail out its MMFs as well as some Altamira funds after it was caught holding tainted asset-backed commercial paper (ABCP) in the wake of the U.S. sub-prime mortgage crash.

The Canadian Securities Administrators (CSA), which brings together all the provincial regulators, announced in September 2008 that it was looking into the extent to which Canadian MMFs might be exposed to high-risk U.S. debt securities, such as short-term notes issued by failed Lehman Brothers and Washington Mutual. The "fact-finding review," as it was called, was conducted in association with the Investment Industry Regulatory Organization of Canada (IIROC), which has oversight responsibility for brokerage houses.

The announcement came after the U.S. government had to step in and guarantee MMFs in that country for losses up to $50 billion after the giant Reserve Primary Fund "broke the buck"—that is, it reduced its net asset value to less than $1 because of losses due to its position in Lehman Brothers notes. (Canadian MMFs normally have a net asset value of $10.)

The Ontario Securities Commission (OSC) subsequently reported that the MMF review had determined there were "no material issues" that would cause concern. The OSC did not provide any details of the study but the fact is that no Canadian MMF has shown any indication of financial difficulty and none has ever dropped below par. That said, many mutual fund companies have reduced MMF fees and cut sales commissions and trailers because low interest rates threatened to reduce returns to zero or below.

My advice is not to automatically assume a specific money market fund is safe. Ask your financial adviser (or the fund company itself if you don't have an adviser) what type of assets are held by the MMF you are considering. Some funds are heavily invested in notes issued by small companies that could be at risk if another financial crisis materializes. If you are not satisfied with the quality of the assets in the fund, switch to another MMF or to a high-interest savings account, which will be covered by deposit insurance.

The safest MMFs are those that invest only in federal or provincial treasury bills or government-guaranteed securities. Most of the major banks offer T-bill funds.

Safety is obviously a priority when it comes to choosing an MMF, but there are other considerations. Not all money market funds are created equal. They may look alike, in the sense that they all have a fixed price of $10 and they all invest in short-term securities. But that's where the similarities end. In fact, there are some very good money market funds, some very bad ones, and a whole lot of mediocre ones. Obviously, you want a good one, so here's what to look for.

No sales commission. Never pay a sales commission to buy or sell money market fund units. There are plenty of good no-load funds around. I once received an email from a distraught investor whose adviser had put his money into two MMFs on a deferred sales charge (DSC) basis. That meant that if he wanted to withdraw cash within the first six years of holding, he would be dinged with a redemption charge. He blamed himself for not paying closer attention, but I blamed his financial adviser, who had obviously acted in his own interest (he got a sales commission) and not in the interest of his client. Don't allow yourself to fall into that trap. MMFs should be commission-free, in and out.

Low fees. Returns on money market funds are historically quite low, so it's important to select a fund that will give you the most bang for your buck. This means avoiding funds with high management expense ratios (MERs). These ratios represent the cost to the fund of management fees and expenses, and they come right off your return. For example, if an MMF generates a gross profit of 2 percent in a given year and has an MER of 0.5 percent, your return is 1.5 percent. But if the MER is 1.5 percent (and some are even higher), your return is only 0.5 percent. Don't have your pocket picked in this way!

When interest rates start to rise again, money market funds will be worth considering for a TFSA. But until then, look at other options.

However you decide to build your emergency fund within a TFSA, always remember the two most important principles: Make sure that your money is safe and that you can get at it quickly if needed.

ACTION SUMMARY

1. Every family should have an emergency fund. A TFSA offers an ideal way to build one.
2. Choose an investment that offers both safety and quick access to your money if it is needed.
3. Avoid GICs or any other security that locks you in for a long time.
4. If you invest in a money market fund at some point, select one that has no sales commissions and low ongoing fees.

6
TFSAs or RRSPs: Which to Choose?

The first question many people are going to ask about TFSAs is whether they should use a Tax-Free Savings Account or an RRSP for retirement saving.

There's no easy answer. TFSAs provide a valuable new option for retirement planning, but how they are best used will depend on each person's circumstances.

To begin with, it's important to understand that TFSAs and RRSPs are two different creatures from a tax and savings perspective. In the jargon of economists, TFSAs are so-called TEE plans—taxed, exempt, exempt. That means the money going into the plan has already been taxed, but earnings within a TFSA are tax-exempt, as are all withdrawals.

In contrast, RRSPs are so-called EET plans—exempt, exempt, taxed. Contributions are tax-free because they generate an offsetting deduction. Investment income earned within an RRSP is also tax-free. But all the money that comes out is taxed at your marginal rate, regardless of its source. That means you'll pay more tax on capital gains and dividends earned within an RRSP than you would if those same profits were generated in a non-registered account.

In the Budget Papers that explained the TFSA concept in detail, the Department of Finance included an example that suggested there is no after-tax advantage in using either TFSAs or RRSPs for retirement savings. Based on their assumptions, both produced the same net after-tax return and both were equally superior to saving in a non-registered account. See below for the illustration they used.[1]

Net Proceeds from Saving in a TFSA
Relative to Other Savings Vehicles

	TFSA	RRSP	Unregistered savings
Pre-tax income	$1000	$1000	$1000
Tax (40% rate)	$ 400	–	$ 400
Net contribution[1]	$ 600	$1000	$ 600
Investment income (20 years at 5.5%)	$1151	$1918	$ 707[2]
Gross proceeds (Net contribution + investment income)	$1751	$2918	$1307
Tax (40% rate)	–	$1167	–
Net proceeds	$1751	$1751	$1307
Net annual after-tax rate of return[3] (%)	5.5	5.5	4.0

1. Forgone consumption (saving) is $600 in all cases. In the RRSP case, the person contributes $1000 but receives a $400 reduction in tax, thereby sacrificing net consumption of $600.
2. For unregistered saving case, tax rate on investment income is 28%, representing a weighted average tax rate on an investment portfolio comprising 30% dividends, 30% capital gains, and 40% interest.
3. Measured in relation to forgone consumption of $600. Assumes annual nominal pre-tax rate of return is 5.5% invested for 20 years.

This example assumes a contribution of $1000 to each of three different accounts—a TFSA, an RRSP, and an unregistered investment plan. But it is important to read the first footnote to the table to understand the rationale the Department of Finance used for the after-tax rate-of-return calculation. The figure is not based on the amount invested but rather on what Finance defines as "forgone consumption." This is the amount actually saved.

In all cases, the investor starts with a gross $1000. With the TFSA and the unregistered account, $400 is taken by taxes, leaving $600 in savings. That's straightforward enough, but the RRSP calculation is more complex: It appears at first glance that $1000 is the amount saved because that's what is paid into the plan and no tax is assessed because of the deduction generated. But the accepted way to make apples-to-apples comparisons in such situations is to examine it from the perspective of how much money a person could have spent if he or she had not made an investment. Using this approach, the "forgone consumption" is $600 in all cases. So the calculation of returns in all three scenarios is based on $600, although that number does not show up on the net contribution line in the RRSP column. For consistency, I'll stay with Finance's approach in the analysis that follows.

Referring to the Finance table, you'll see that it shows the average annual compound rate of return for both a TFSA and an RRSP is 5.5 percent and the tax rate going in and coming out is 40 percent. But if you change those basic assumptions, the end result can be quite different. Let's manipulate the numbers and consider the various outcomes. We'll begin by assuming that the contributor's marginal tax rate is lower in retirement than when she was working. We'll consider only a TFSA versus an RRSP because the results in an unregistered account don't change. Here is what happens, again using the "forgone consumption" of $600 as the base.

Net Proceeds from Saving in a TFSA Relative to an RRSP When the Final Tax Rate Is Lower

	TFSA	RRSP
Pre-tax income	$1000	$1000
Tax (40% rate)	$ 400	–
Net contribution	$ 600	$1000
Investment income (20 years at 5.5%)	$1151	$1918
Gross proceeds (Net contribution + investment income)	$1751	$2918
Tax (30% rate)	–	$ 875
Net proceeds	$1751	$2043
Net annual after-tax rate of return (%)	5.5	6.3

Explanatory notes from the table on page 56 also apply here.

In this case, as the table shows, the RRSP is clearly the better choice. It produces an average annual compound rate of return of 6.3 percent over 20 years compared to 5.5 percent for a TFSA. This means that higher-income people who expect their tax rate to be lower after retirement should top up their RRSPs first before investing in a TFSA.

Now let's see what happens when the tax rate after retirement is higher than when a person was working.

Net Proceeds from Saving in a TFSA Relative an RRSP When the Final Tax Rate Is Higher

	TFSA	RRSP
Pre-tax income	$1000	$1000
Tax (30% rate)	$ 300	–
Net contribution	$ 700	$1000
Investment income (20 years at 5.5%)	$1342	$1918
Gross proceeds (Net contribution + investment income)	$2042	$2918
Tax (40% rate)	–	$1167
Net proceeds	$2042	$1751
Net annual after-tax rate of return (%)	5.5	4.7

To sum up, if you expect your tax rate after retirement to be less than it is now, top up your RRSP before opening a TFSA. If you expect your tax rate after retirement to be higher than it is now, saving in a TFSA will produce a better return than making an RRSP contribution.

The C.D. Howe Analysis

In January 2010, the C.D. Howe Institute released a position paper by Alexandre Laurin and Finn Poschmann that examined the RRSP/TFSA issue in depth. One of its main conclusions was that even though TFSAs are not marketed as a retirement savings vehicle, for many people they are more tax-efficient than RRSPs "because the effective rate of tax payable on retirement income is often higher than that imposed on regular income during working life."[2]

The study said that, although most people expect their marginal tax rate will be lower after they retire this is not necessarily the case. The authors acknowledged that it is easier for older workers to estimate their marginal effective tax rate (METR) after retirement than it is for young people with decades of saving time ahead of them but found that some general rules can be applied.

"At low income levels, METRs at retirement significantly exceed those of working life," the report concluded. "This is caused mainly by the GIS clawback rate for seniors, which may be 50 or 75 percent, depending on family configuration."

Somewhat surprisingly, they also concluded that where you live affects the decision on whether to use an RRSP or a TFSA for retirement saving.

"In Alberta in particular, where the tax system is less geared-to-income and simpler than in other provinces, individuals who are currently close to retirement appear better off putting their incremental retirement saving in a TFSA-like arrangement, rather than in a tax-deferred vehicle, no matter their target income-replacement rate," they wrote.

To address the situation, the authors recommended that the government give Canadians more flexibility to decide whether to allocate their retirement savings to TFSAs or RRSPs. One way to achieve this would be to combine the contribution limits for both programs and allow people to make their own allocations. As things stand right now, RRSPs offer more contribution room to anyone whose earned income exceeds about $30,500 per year.

Why Pension Plan Members Need TFSAs

Anyone who belongs to a pension plan loses RRSP contribution room because of the "pension adjustment" (PA). This is a complex calculation that takes into account the amount contributed to a pension plan by you and your employer, as well as the retirement benefit you will eventually receive. The more generous the plan, the higher the PA will be.

Anyone with a defined benefit pension plan (one that provides guaranteed retirement income based on a combination of salary and years of service) is likely to have a high PA. People in higher-income brackets may find they have little or no RRSP room left after the PA has been deducted.

In this situation, TFSAs offer a valuable alternative for supplementing pension income. By making the maximum possible contribution each year, you can build a tax-paid nest egg that will provide extra income that can be used for travel, a home in the sunbelt, helping your kids buy a first home, a grandchild's post-secondary education, or anything else you may want to do after you stop work.

There's another reason to set up a TFSA to add to your retirement savings: It's a form of pension insurance. In the past, North Americans took their pension plans for granted. Not anymore. In recent years, many pension plans have been forced to cut benefits because the funding was no longer there to support them.

Financially troubled US Airways had to cut pension benefits for its pilots by as much as 70 percent. Other major American airlines have sought to do the same, as did Air Canada while it was under creditor protection (it didn't succeed). Bethlehem Steel went into bankruptcy, leaving behind US$3.6 billion in unpaid obligations to its plan.

The Pension Benefits Guaranty Corporation (PBGC), which provides limited support to U.S. pensioners who have had their payments cut or suspended, reported in its 2011 annual report that it was paying an average of US$458 million a month to 873,000 retirees whose plans had failed. At that point it was also on the hook for another 628,000 workers who had not yet retired.[3]

The introduction to the report written by PBGC director Josh Gotbaum warned that retirement security in the United States is in trouble. He was particularly critical of the move by employers to defined contribution (DC) pension plans, which "may force individual employees to become their own retirement and investment experts; as a result, many save too little, invest it in ways that generate a lower return, and often use the savings for things other than retirement."

Mr. Gotbaum cited a 2009 report by the National Institute on Retirement Security that found 83 percent of people surveyed are concerned about their retirement. One of the main reasons for this is the escalating number of pension plan failures. In fiscal 2011, the PBGC reported that 152 underfunded single-employer pension plans were terminated, increasing the organization's total obligations to US$107 billion. At that point, it faced a net deficit of US$26 billion.

The bottom line is that pension plans in the United States are failing at an alarming rate, putting increasing pressure on an already cash-strapped government agency.

This isn't just an American problem. It has happened here, and even the biggest Canadian plans are not immune. But in Canada, we have no equivalent to the PBGC. That means there is no government agency to protect you if your own pension plan runs into financial trouble. (Ontario has a provincial program, but the benefits it covers are minimal.)

In September 2008, the Ontario Teachers' Pension Plan, which has more than $100 billion in assets, asked its members to give up part of their inflation-protection indexing to help deal with a $12.7-billion funding deficit.[4] If it can happen to teachers, who's safe?

The message is, take nothing for granted. TFSAs provide an opportunity to backstop your pension plan with what amounts to your own pension insurance policy. Take advantage of it.

Lower-Income Canadians

As we saw in Chapter 2, the primary rationale for the C.D. Howe Institute's strong advocacy of TFSAs was to provide an alternative retirement savings program that would better meet the needs of low-income people.

In all its reports on the subject, the Institute was critical of the way in which low-income savers were penalized by government policies when the time came to draw on their RRSP or RRIF accounts. The most scathing denouncement was contained in Dr. Richard Shillington's 2003 paper, *New Poverty Traps: Means Testing and Modest-Income Seniors*.

"The primary beneficiary of this saving will be the federal

and provincial governments because most of the income from it will be confiscated by income-tested programs and income taxes," Shillington wrote. "To the extent that these households have been misled, they have been defrauded."[5]

The report makes a clear distinction between the value of RRSP saving for higher-income Canadians, who will ultimately benefit from their plans, and lower-income people, who will not. Shillington's message was that all those with less than $100,000 in retirement assets are "futile savers" because they will probably need financial support from governments after they stop work. Those benefits will be reduced or even eliminated if there is any income from RRSPs and RRIFs. (Remember: Every dollar in income from one of those plans reduces a Guaranteed Income Supplement benefit by 50 cents once the $3500 exemption has been exceeded.)

Using a TFSA instead of an RRSP eliminates that problem, at least on the federal level. The federal government has ensured that TFSA withdrawals are not treated as income, nor will they be taken into account when calculating eligibility for GIS, tax credits, Employment Insurance, and so forth.

Clearly, anyone with a modest income should favour TFSAs over RRSPs for retirement-savings purposes, even when the amounts being put aside are small.

No Earned Income

You cannot make an RRSP contribution unless you have what the government calls "earned income." Mostly, this is money earned from employment, but some other types of income, such as rents and alimony, also qualify. Investment income does not qualify as earned income, nor do pension payments, whether from the government or from a private plan.

If you don't have any earned income, or if the amount is small, TFSAs become your retirement-savings vehicle by default. That's because you don't need any earned income to make a TFSA contribution.

Years ago, the typical Canadian family had one wage earner, usually the husband. The wife remained at home and raised the couple's children. Such families are less common today, but they still exist. In this situation, the wife is not able to save independently for her retirement through an RRSP because she has no earned income. If the wife has no earned income, the husband can make a spousal contribution on her behalf, but spousal RRSPs have significant restrictions on the ability to withdraw funds.

Now she has an option: a TFSA. She does not need to have earned income to set up a personal retirement account. If she has some money of her own (perhaps from an inheritance from her parents), she can contribute some of it to the plan. Alternatively, her husband can give her the money to contribute, since income attribution rules will not apply in this case.

When RRSPs Are Better

There are some situations in which an RRSP is a better option than a TFSA—in fact, it may be the only choice. One example is a child or teenager with earned income. You must be 18 or older to open a TFSA, but there is no age limit for RRSPs. As long as a person has earned income, that person can have an RRSP account.

Most people don't realize this, so they pass up opportunities to encourage their children to put some of their earnings, however modest they may be, into an RRSP. For example, my granddaughter had a job at Canada's Wonderland, an amusement park north of Toronto, during the summer when she was 16. Her wages were modest, but they qualified as earned income for RRSP purposes. She was too young to open a TFSA, but she could contribute 18 percent of her earned income (the maximum allowed) to an RRSP. And she could defer claiming the tax deduction until she is working full-time and the deduction will be more worthwhile. Meanwhile, the money will be compounding inside her RRSP.

She earned about $2800 over the summer. That allowed her to contribute $500 to an RRSP. At the time, she had 49 years before she would reach age 65. At an average annual growth rate of 5 percent, that $500 would grow more than 10 times, to $5460.67, at the end of that time. It's just one more example of the magic of compounding.

First-Time Homebuyers

One of the most popular features of RRSPs is the Home Buyers' Plan (HBP). This program allows first-time homebuyers to borrow up to $25,000 from an RRSP interest-free and to pay the money back over 15 years. Hundreds of thousands of Canadians have made use of it since the plan was introduced in 1992, originally as a temporary measure to help a beleaguered housing market. Now aspiring homeowners face the dilemma of whether to use an RRSP or a TFSA as the savings vehicle for their down payment.

An RRSP allows you to reach your financial goal more quickly because you do not pay tax on RRSP contributions (you get an offsetting tax deduction) and your money therefore accumulates faster. Take a look at the following chart. It shows how much money would be accumulated in each plan based on $3500 a year in before-tax income. I've assumed an annual rate of return of 5 percent and for purposes of the TFSA contributions a marginal tax rate of 30 percent on the $3500.

Home Ownership Savings: RRSPs versus TFSAs

Year	RRSP	TFSA
1	$3675	$2573
2	$7534	$5274
3	$11,585	$8110
4	$15,840	$11,088
5	$20,307	$14,215
6	$24,997	$17,498

At the end of six years, you will have accumulated almost $25,000 in the RRSP and can take maximum advantage of the HBP. The value of the TFSA, however, is only $17,498 because you were only able to contribute $2450 a year after tax. It will be an additional two years before the TFSA reaches the $25,000 level, by which time you'll have your house.

If you had to withdraw the money outright from the RRSP to buy the home, it would be a different story because the $25,000 would be taxed coming out. But with the HBP (as well as the Lifelong Learning Plan, which allows interest-free RRSP loans for continuing education), no tax is assessed on withdrawals as long as the loan is repaid on schedule or faster.

So, if saving for a first home is your number-one priority, the RRSP is the best way to do it. If you want to move even faster, use your RRSP refund to open a TFSA and save both ways.

Large Contributions

Because of the low contribution limits on TFSAs, big savers are better off using RRSPs because they can shelter more money from taxes. The maximum RRSP contribution for the 2013 tax year is $23,820, more than four times the amount you can put into a TFSA.

Of course, you're allowed to do both—the two types of plans can be used in tandem to build a supersized retirement nest egg.

ACTION SUMMARY

1. Contribute to an RRSP before a TFSA if you expect to be taxed at a lower rate after retirement. If your tax rate is likely to be higher than it is now, use the TFSA first.

2. If you are a member of a pension plan, contribute to TFSAs to supplement your retirement savings, especially if you have little or no RRSP room.

3. If you are planning to buy a house, save for your down payment in an RRSP rather than a TFSA and make use of the RRSP Home Buyers' Plan.

7

Tax Relief for Seniors

Although statistics tell us that many retired Canadians live below the poverty line, a lot of retirees are doing very well for themselves.

According to preliminary data published by the Canada Revenue Agency, about 4.1 million Canadians over age 65 filed tax returns for 2010 (the latest year for which figures were available at the time of writing). Of these, almost 2.2 million (53 percent) reported taxable income, in the amount of $148.8 billion. That works out to an average of over $67,000 per taxable filer.[1] Clearly, these folks are doing all right.

The other side of the coin is that almost half of older people (47 percent) live on incomes that are so low they don't even meet the minimum threshold for paying tax. In reality, the percentage is probably much higher because the data only covers tax filers. How many more seniors don't bother to submit a return because their incomes are low or non-existent?

Compare that with the average income of tax-paying retirees and it's immediately apparent that there is a huge gap between the two groups. TFSAs won't bridge that chasm, although over time they may reduce the income disparity by giving lower-income people more incentive to save. But the first ones to benefit are those on the higher-income side of the retirement divide.

I frequently receive emails from older readers who are angry because the payments from their Registered Retirement Income Funds (RRIFs) are taxed at such a high rate (RRIFs are the programs used to generate income from RRSP savings). Some are so outraged, they say that if they had realized how much tax they'd have to pay they never would have bothered saving for retirement in the first place.

My response to such complaints is always the same: You're lucky. Anyone who has to pay high taxes does so because he or she enjoys above-average income. There are worse things to worry about in retirement than making too much money. I doubt many of the complainers would want to trade places with someone at the other end of the income scale.

That said, I understand the desire of these folks to cut their tax bills. And as long as it can be done legally, I encourage them to go ahead. TFSAs offer several ways to achieve that goal. The savings aren't necessarily dramatic, but every little bit helps.

Advance Planning

As we saw in the last chapter, anyone who expects their tax rate to be higher in retirement should be saving in a TFSA rather than an RRSP. There are a number of situations in which that might happen. Here are three examples.

You start a business. A growing number of people move on to a new career after they stop working. This may be anything from consulting to dog breeding. When combined with pension and investment income, the additional cash flow could push these people into a higher tax bracket.

Consider the example of a B.C. government worker with the provincial Ministry of Small Business and Revenue. Her pre-retirement taxable income was $70,000, and her marginal tax rate was about 30 percent. She retires at 65 with a pension equal to 75 percent of her salary, or $52,500. She draws CPP benefits of $11,800 a year and Old Age Security of $6500, bringing the total to $70,800—slightly more than when she was working.

She then decides to start a tax-preparation service for small companies. It turns out to be highly successful and generates an additional $25,000 in net income. Her marginal tax rate has just jumped to more than 38 percent, based on 2012 rates!

If this woman has saved any money in an RRSP, she will have to pay more tax when it comes out than the value of the refund she received when she made the contribution. Had she put the same amount into a TFSA, she would have ended up ahead.

You receive a windfall. Everyone dreams of winning a lottery, but the most likely windfall you'll receive is an inheritance. As baby boomers approach retirement, many will lose their last surviving parent and the estate will pass to the next generation. Even after the government takes its tax cut, billions of dollars' worth of savings, real estate, and insurance will end up in the hands of adult children who are themselves close to leaving the workforce.

In some cases, the inheritance may be worth hundreds of thousands of dollars or even more. When invested, this money will generate returns that, when added to other income, will move the heirs into higher tax brackets. To illustrate, a $500,000 inheritance that earns 5 percent a year will add $25,000 to a person's income. That's enough to push an Ontario resident who had been receiving $60,000 a year in taxable income from a marginal tax rate of 31.15 percent all the way to 39.41 percent (2012 rates). While there won't be enough TFSA room available for several years to shelter a large inheritance, anyone who anticipates receiving a bequest should open a plan now and be ready to move as much money as possible into it when the time comes.

You plan to move to a higher-tax province. Consider the case of a Nova Scotian who went to Alberta to work in the oil sands industry. He has made good money, slightly more than $100,000 a year. But because Alberta tax rates are so low, his marginal tax rate is only 36 percent. Now he's retiring and wants to return to Halifax where his family still lives. He'll receive less income in retirement—his pension, CPP, OAS, and a small amount of investment income will add up to about $87,000 a year in taxable income. But because tax rates are much higher in Nova Scotia, his marginal rate will actually rise to 42.67 percent.

In all these situations, starting a TFSA during the working years will produce better post-retirement after-tax results than an RRSP.

After You've Retired

After you've fully retired, the TFSA/RRSP dilemma may still come into play. We are allowed to have RRSPs and to make contributions to them until the end of the year in which we turn 71. Even retirees under 71 with no earned income can take advantage of this situation if they have unused carry-forward room, which many do. Check the My Account feature on the Canada Revenue Agency website to find out whether you do too. If you have not registered for this service, I suggest you do so. Go to www.cra-arc.gc.ca and click on the My Account link.

But even if you have RRSP contribution room and are still eligible to have a plan, is it worthwhile using it now that TFSAs are available?

Perhaps, but you need to look at the situation carefully. For starters, how much money is involved? You can contribute only $5500 a year to a TFSA. If you have more unused RRSP contribution room than your TFSA limit and you have the necessary cash, you should make use of the RRSP. Remember, the more money you can tax-shelter and the sooner you can do it, the better.

Next, consider whether you expect your tax rate to be lower, higher, or about the same after age 71. If it is likely to be higher, forget about the RRSP unless you would rather exchange a small tax deduction now for a higher tax bill later. If you anticipate no change, it's a toss-up, but since you can only keep the RRSP for a few years longer anyway, you may want to go right to a TFSA.

You should also look at your exposure to the Old Age Security clawback, which cuts in when net income exceeds $69,562 (2012 rates). This onerous surtax grabs back 15 cents of every dollar of net income that exceeds the threshold. And that's on top of your regular tax rate. The effect is that a Quebec resident who receives OAS payments and has taxable income of $70,000 is being socked at a marginal rate of more than 53 percent! Since RRSP and RRIF payments count as income but TFSA withdrawals do not, anyone who expects to be subject to the clawback should opt for a TFSA.

For modest-income retirees (anyone earning less than $30,000 a year), it's a no-brainer. Choose the TFSA over an RRSP. This ensures you won't compromise your eligibility for the Guaranteed Income Supplement or various federal tax credits.

Most people over the age of 71 won't have to choose between a TFSA and an RRSP, but there are exceptions. Suppose a 72-year-old married woman (who can no longer hold an RRSP) has earned income and/or unused carry-forward room. Her disabled husband is 69 and is therefore still RRSP-eligible. In this case, the woman has a choice: She can make a contribution to a spousal RRSP or put money into a TFSA.

The key consideration here is what her husband's tax rate is likely to be in the future compared to her current marginal rate. In this case, the odds are that the husband's rate will be very low—in fact, he may not have to pay any tax at all once he claims the personal and disability credits. So the spousal RRSP would be the right choice—she gets a deduction now, and the money comes out of the husband's plan later as income in his hands. That means it will be taxed at a low rate or perhaps not at all.

RRIF/LIF Withdrawals

Once an RRSP is converted to a RRIF or a life income fund (LIF: a locked-in account funded by pension plan money), the federal government requires that a minimum amount be taken out of the plan annually. This is based on a percentage of the market value of the plan on January 1 of each year. The minimum percentage you are required to withdraw increases with age; at 70, it is 5 percent, but by the time you reach 75, it is up to 7.85 percent.

Canadians who have other sources of income, such as an employer pension, frequently complain that these forced withdrawals put them in a position of taking out more money than they need, thereby pushing them into a higher tax bracket. The tax implications are especially onerous in cases where RRIF/LIF withdrawals add enough to a person's income to move them over the OAS clawback threshold. The pension-splitting rules may ease the tax situation for some couples, but most retirees would prefer to have greater flexibility in deciding how much to take out of a RRIF or LIF each year.

Two decades from now, TFSAs should have eased the problem because they allow future generations the flexibility to diversify their retirement savings, thereby reducing the dependence on taxable RRIFs. But what about today?

Unfortunately, TFSAs do nothing to ease the immediate tax bite of RRIF/LIF withdrawals. What they can do is to shelter future investment income from the tax folks.

Prior to TFSAs, there was no inexpensive tax-shelter program for Canadians over age 71. Universal life policies offer tax protection, but they are expensive, and if you don't already have one, your health may disqualify you. TFSAs change the landscape.

Retirees can now move $5500 a year (so $11,000 per couple) of unneeded RRIF/LIF withdrawals into TFSA accounts. Yes, they'll still pay tax on the money as it comes out of the RRIF/LIF, but at least they will be able to ensure they will not have to pay any more tax on the future investment income they earn.

Since older people have a shorter life expectancy, the benefits of TFSAs aren't as great as for people in their twenties. However, Statistics Canada tells us that a Canadian male aged 65 can expect to live another 18.5 years, while a woman in the same age group can expect to survive another 21.6 years.[2]

So let's assume that a woman who is now age 70 starts contributing $5500 a year from unneeded RRIF withdrawals to a TFSA. She continues to do this for the next five years, during which time the investment income accrues at an average annual compound rate of 5 percent. By age 75, she has a tax-free nest egg worth $31,911. At this point, she finds that she needs the full amount of her RRIF withdrawal to live on, so she stops contributing her RRIF withdrawals to the TFSA and simply allows the money in the TFSA to continue compounding. By the time she is 80, the TFSA will be worth $40,727. At age 85, the woman will find that her TFSA has grown to $51,980. At this point, her RRIF may be almost depleted, but she now has the TFSA to fall back on and she won't need to withdraw as much to live on because no tax will be withheld. If she doesn't need the money in the TFSA, it will make a nice inheritance for her children or grandchildren.

So even if you are in your seventies, don't ignore the tax-saving potential of these new plans. Sure, it would have been nice if they'd been available when you entered the workforce so many years ago, but better late than never.

ACTION SUMMARY

1. If you are not yet retired, give careful thought to what your income is likely to be after you stop work and how much tax you will pay. It will help you decide whether to make any more RRSP contributions.
2. If you plan to move after you retire, check the tax rates in the province to which you are relocating.
3. Invest any unneeded RRIF withdrawal money in a TFSA, up to the annual limit.

8
Education Savings

Which type of savings plan should you choose for a child's or grandchild's university education? At first glance, there are a lot of similarities between Tax-Free Savings Accounts (TFSAs) and Registered Education Savings Plans (RESPs).

Both are funded with tax-paid money—you don't receive a deduction for your contributions.

Both tax-shelter investment income earned within the plan.

Both allow the tax-free withdrawal of contributions at any time.

Both have a contribution year-end of December 31, unlike RRSPs which allow you 60 days after the end of a calendar year to get your money into the plan.

But that's where the resemblance ends. RESPs come with several strings and conditions, as well as with government-sponsored savings incentives. TFSAs are much more flexible, but Ottawa doesn't kick in any extra cash to encourage you to use them.

So the answer of whether to choose a TFSA or an RESP for education savings is not as clear-cut as you might expect.

Registered Education Savings Plans (RESPs)

Let's begin by looking at the pros and cons of RESPs. These plans have been around for years but were seldom used until the federal government decided to give them a boost by creating the Canada Education Savings Grant (CESG). This is a program operated by Human Resources and Skills Development Canada that adds a 20 percent bonus to your annual RESP contribution to a maximum of $500 a year. The lifetime limit is $7200 per child, and there are no income restrictions on these grants. They are paid directly into the RESP. A child is entitled to the CESG from birth through to age 17.

There is a bonus amount for lower-income families. If net family income is $42,707 or less (2012 figures), the CESG may be increased by a maximum of $100 per child, to $600 a year. For families with net income in the range of $42,707 to $85,414, the maximum annual CESG is $550 annually. The $7,200 lifetime maximum still applies.

Another support program for low-income families is the Canada Learning Bond, which is worth up to $2,000 for the RESP. Alberta and Quebec offer supplemental programs that can add to the plan.

CESG and Canada Learning Bond payments are made directly to the RESP, not to the parent or the child personally.

These grants are paid until the year the child (technically known as the "plan beneficiary") turns 17. But there are some conditions. Grants will be paid only on behalf of beneficiaries who are 16 or 17 if the RESP was set up before they turned 16 and a minimum of $100 a year was contributed to the plan for four years. The other option is to put at least $2000 into the plan before the beneficiary turns age 16 (which could all be contributed in a single year or spread out).

What this boils down to is that, for older children to qualify for the CESG, the RESP must be set up before the end of the calendar year in which the child turns 15 and the required contributions must be made.

The CESG is a powerful incentive to use RESPs and can add thousands of dollars to the end value of a plan. For example, suppose a parent opens an RESP for a newborn and contributes enough money each year to earn the basic grant. In the child's fifteenth year, the maximum lifetime grant of $7200 will be reached. If the money in the RESP earns 6 percent annually, by the time the child is 18, the added value of the CESG plus accumulated earnings will be more than $14,000.

No wonder RESPs have become more popular in recent years!

Another advantage offered by these plans is contribution flexibility. In the past, parents or grandparents were restricted to a maximum annual contribution of $4000. Now there is no annual maximum—the only limitation is that the lifetime amount contributed on behalf of any one child cannot exceed $50,000. (Remember, however, that only the first $2500 contributed qualifies for the CESG in that year.) You are allowed to make contributions until the plan beneficiary turns 31.

Now let's consider the drawbacks of RESPs.

Income taxed on withdrawal. Although contributions to an RESP can be withdrawn tax-free at any time, investment income earned within a plan is taxed when it comes out. These are called educational assistance payments (EAPs). Fortunately, such withdrawals are deemed to be income received by the student, not the contributor. Since a university student is unlikely to have much income from other sources, tax payable on RESP withdrawals may not be significant— indeed, the student may have no taxable income at all once the tuition and education tax credits are applied.

Money must be used for education. The rules governing RESP withdrawals are fairly loose. As long as the end use relates to post-secondary education (college, university, trade schools, CEGEPs, etc.), almost anything goes. Withdrawals can be used to pay for tuition, residence, books, travel, athletics, even a computer. And there is nothing in the rules that says the beneficiary must go to a Canadian university; an RESP can be used to finance a Harvard education if the student can gain admission.

The one major limitation is a ceiling of $5,000 that can be withdrawn as an educational assistance payment during the first thirteen weeks a student is enrolled in a qualifying educational program. After that, there is no limit on the amount that can be withdrawn as long as the student continues to attend school.

Penalties if a child quits school. If the beneficiary does not go on to post-secondary studies, there's a problem. This is where the real downside of RESPs comes into play.

Contributors face an extremely high tax penalty if the plan beneficiary decides not to pursue a post-secondary education. These plans are specifically intended for education saving, and the government hits contributors with hefty taxes if things don't work out that way (most RESPs must be wound up by their 35th-anniversary date).

You might argue that this is inherently unfair. After all, it is not the fault of the parents if their daughter decides that university isn't her thing or if her marks aren't good enough to gain admission. They did everything they were supposed to, dutifully cutting back their spending so they could put money aside for her schooling. Why should they be penalized when she decides she would rather take a job at the local mall or travel around the world? After all, the government doesn't punish RRSP investors if they don't use the money to fund their retirement.

If a child decides not to go on to post-secondary education, the cost to the plan and the contributor can amount to thousands of dollars. The contributor may withdraw the contributions tax-free but will have to repay all the money received from the Canada Education Savings Grant and the Canada Learning Bond to the government.

The money that remains in the RESP will consist of the investment income earned over the years. In a case where $2500 a year was contributed to a plan over 18 years that earned 6 percent annually, the investment earnings will amount to almost $37,000.

Once the contributor takes this money out of an RESP that is not used by the beneficiary, it is called an accumulated income payment (AIP). If the contributing parent or grandparent has an RRSP and enough contribution room available, he or she can move the AIP there directly without having to pay tax on it (or use a spousal plan). But if an RRSP transfer is not feasible, the tax hit is fierce.

In that case, the AIP will be added to your regular income for the year in which it is received. That means it will be taxed at your marginal rate. But the government wants more. You'll be hit with an extra 20 percent penalty on top of that (12 percent in Quebec), which pushes the effective tax rate to almost confiscatory levels.

To put this in perspective, let's look at the case of an Ontario father who has a taxable income of $45,000 a year. The family scrimped and saved in an RESP to send their son (an only child) to university, but he was academically challenged and dropped out of high school in his senior year. The parents were not only disappointed with his decision but were left with the problem of winding up the RESP. After repaying the government grants and withdrawing their principal, the parents found the RESP had $20,000 remaining in it. Since neither parent had any RRSP contribution room available, the money had to be withdrawn as an AIP.

Using 2012 rates, the normal tax payable on the $20,000 withdrawal would be $6230, based on the father's regular income. But the 20 percent penalty would add $4000 to the bill, bringing the total to $10,230. That works out to an effective tax rate of 51.15 percent on the AIP. There is no reasonable justification for this, but it is how the system operates. The result is that RESPs are something of a gamble, despite all the government support.

Scholarship trusts. There is one other risk to RESPs that relates directly to the type of plan used. Scholarship trusts have aggressively marketed RESP programs for years, and some have been quite successful. Students who meet the qualifications and use the plans to go through university can receive generous grants.

But the trusts charge hefty upfront fees, and families that decide to drop out of the plan early can end up losing thousands of dollars. So they carry a double risk—first, that the child may not go on to college and, second, that the parents may not be able to keep up with the payment schedule.

Tax-Free Savings Accounts and Education Savings

There are no bells and whistles if you decide to use a TFSA rather than an RESP to save for a child's education. You get no government support—the only money in the plan is what you contribute.

But there is also no risk of penalties if the youngster does not go on to post-secondary education. The money that accumulates in a TFSA can be used for any purpose at all. The government won't sock it to you if your child or grandchild decides not to go to university.

This flexibility means that there is no pressure on a child to do something he or she doesn't want to do. It also means that the money you've accumulated can be used for some other purpose, such as providing a down payment on a first home or paying for a wedding.

What makes the decision so difficult is that there is no way of knowing when a child is young whether he or she will eventually go on to post-secondary education. Surprisingly, there appears to be no data that tells us what percentage of children in Canada who start elementary school eventually proceed to some form of post-secondary education. When I put that question to the Ontario Ministry of Education, I was informed by a researcher that "the requested data will be available starting 2017–2018 as the ministry started collecting elementary student level data in the 2005–2006 school year for the first time." That's not much help to a parent who is trying to decide right now whether to risk opening an RESP.

A report published in 2006 by Colleges Ontario found that 52 percent of Ontario high school graduates enrolled in college or university.[1] However, this refers only to students who actually finished high school.

If the federal government were to eliminate the 20-percent tax penalty, parents would not be faced with such a difficult choice. But unless that happens, Canadians will be forced to make a decision when a child is very young that they may come to regret years later.

Which to Choose?

From a strictly financial perspective, an RESP is the better choice if the plan beneficiary is young. The following table compares the value of an RESP and a TFSA at the end of various time frames. It assumes an annual contribution of $2500 plus the payment of the basic CESG to the RESP at a rate of $500 a year to a maximum of $7200. The average annual compound rate of return is 6 percent.

RESPs vs. TFSAs (1)

Years	RESP	TFSA	RESP gain
5	$17,926	$14,938	+$2988
10	$41,915	$34,929	+$6986
15	$73,700	$61,681	+$12,019
20	$113,565	$97,482	+$16,083

Assumption: Average annual compound rate of return is 6%.

As you can see, the RESP offers a significant financial advantage, and the longer the plan is in existence, the greater the differential. However, the only reason the RESP generates more money is the contribution from the Canada Education Savings Grant. Without the CESG, the end result for both plans would be the same.

But remember, if a child does not have an RESP opened for her before the end of the year she turns 15, she will not be eligible for the CESG. This changes the equation for people who come late to education savings. With the CESG removed from the calculation, the advantage shifts to using a TFSA rather than an RESP for the following reasons.

Same financial result. Both plans will accumulate the same amount of money, assuming equal contributions and rates of return.

No withdrawal restrictions. TFSA savings don't have to be used for education purposes. If the child decides not to go the post-secondary route, the money can be spent on something else or simply left in the plan to accumulate.

No tax on withdrawals. Although the tax rate on most RESP withdrawals will be low or non-existent, TFSA withdrawals are completely tax-free.

However, keep in mind that only $5500 a year can be contributed to a TFSA, whereas there is no annual limit on RESPs. If the goal is to quickly build a large education fund for an older child who is certain to go on to post-secondary education, consider using the two plans in combination.

A TFSA may also be a better choice for people with a lot of money. If the parent or grandparent wants to contribute more than $50,000 to an education savings plan (the maximum allowed per child in an RESP) and the contributions are spread over several years, a TFSA produces a better return in the end.

Let's look at a scenario of a child born in 2013. The parents want to save $5000 a year for her education. Which plan works better? After 10 years, the lifetime RESP maximum is reached and the contributions stop. But since there is no such restriction on TFSAs, the payments continue. The RESP receives the maximum $500 grant each year for 10 years for a total of $5000. (Since there is no accumulated grant room, the parents lose out on the remaining $2200 of CESG payments.) The result is in the following table.

Thanks to the CESG payment, the RESP jumps into an early lead. But after year 10, when contributions cease, the TFSA starts to close the gap. At the end of year 12, the values of both plans are almost equal. After that, the TFSA moves ahead and the gap continues to widen in each subsequent year.

RESPs vs. TFSAs (2)

Years	RESP	TFSA	RESP gain/loss
5	$32,854	$29,877	+$2987
10	$76,844	$69,858	+$6986
15	$102,835	$123,363	-$20,528
20	$137,616	$194,964	-$57,348

Assumption: Average annual compound rate of return is 6%.

However, keep in mind that twice as much money is contributed by the parents or grandparents to the TFSA as to the RESP. The RESP is actually more efficient because of the CESG, even though the amount of money in the plan after 20 years is $57,000 less.

The bottom line is that if the child is eligible for the Canada Education Savings Grant, an RESP is a more efficient way to save for university from a financial perspective. But each family will have to decide whether it is willing to live with the tax risk involved if the student does not choose to pursue post-secondary education.

ACTION SUMMARY

1. For young children, open an RESP instead of a TFSA for education savings because of the added benefit of the CESG. However, be aware of the potential tax risk if the child does not go on to post-secondary education.
2. For older children who do not already have RESPs, use a TFSA to save for their education unless you anticipate making contributions of more than $5500 a year.

9

Save Taxes by Splitting Income

Splitting income between spouses/partners is a great way to save taxes. The problem is that, except in the case of certain types of pensions, there are not many opportunities to do it under our tax laws. This means that Canadian couples end up paying a lot more in taxes than, for example, American couples, who are allowed to file joint returns.

The extra tax we pay can add up to thousands of dollars a year per couple. Take a look at the following table. It shows how much money could be saved in taxes each year by Ontario couples of various income levels if full income splitting were allowed in Canada. The figures assume there is one wage-earner who, under the current system, cannot divide income with the non-working spouse. They show how much could be saved if that were to become possible. The figures are based on 2012 tax rates. I used the online personal tax calculator provided by the accounting firm of Ernst & Young to crunch the numbers.[1]

The table clearly illustrates that if couples were allowed to split all income, the savings would be significant. Moreover, the last column shows that such a change in policy would provide the greatest relief in percentage terms to the lowest-income families, leaving them with more after-tax income. In some cases, this might be enough to remove them from social welfare rolls.

The Effect of Income Splitting

Family taxable income	Tax (current system)	Tax (income splitting)	Tax savings	Reduction
$30,000	$3917	$1516	$2401	61.3%
$40,000	$5962	$3824	$2138	35.9%
$50,000	$8887	$5828	$3059	34.4%
$60,000	$12,002	$7834	$4168	34.7%
$80,000	$18,486	$11,924	$6562	35.5%
$100,000	$26,912	$17,774	$9138	34.0%

Based on 2012 tax rates using Ernst & Young online personal tax calculator.

The Conservative Party has dabbled with income splitting, but only for targeted groups. In 2007, new rules took effect that allowed pension income to be divided between spouses or partners. However, the regulations make the program so complicated that even tax professionals have trouble figuring out the optimum split in individual situations. Tax filers who prepare their own returns should use a software program to help them make the correct calculations.

The Conservatives' 2008 election platform contained a promise to extend income splitting to caregivers of family members with disabilities. However, by the time of the 2011 election, that promise had changed to a Family Caregiver Tax

Credit in the amount of $2000. That's a far cry from income splitting.

The plain fact is that for the great majority of Canadians, income splitting remains an elusive dream.

In addition to limiting income splitting to just a few situations, the Canada Revenue Agency has strict rules that prevent the transfer of assets from one spouse to another (or to minor children) for purposes of dividing investment income. Under these "income attribution" regulations, any dividends, capital gains, or interest earned in this way must be declared for tax purposes by the person who provided the money originally.

For example, suppose a husband wanted to give $50,000 to his wife as a gift. The transfer of money in itself is not illegal and does not attract tax. But now let's assume the wife invests the cash and earns 5 percent on it, which works out to $2500 in the first year. That income must be declared on the husband's tax return, not hers.

TFSAs are a game changer. Over several years, a couple can put together a meaningful income-splitting plan, at least as far as their investments are concerned.

The key that makes this possible is that the Canada Revenue Agency waives the attribution rules when the money is used to invest in a TFSA. Annex 4 of the 2008 Budget Plan states as follows:

> *If an individual transfers property to the individual's spouse or common-law partner, the income tax rules generally treat any income earned on that property as*

income of the individual. An exception to these "attribution rules" will allow individuals to take advantage of the TFSA contribution room available to them using funds provided by their spouse or common-law partner: The rules will not apply to income earned in a TFSA that is derived from such contributions.[2]

This means that even if a wife has no income and no assets, the husband can transfer up to $5500 a year to her (the expected annual maximum contribution after January 1, 2013) to invest in a TFSA. As her plan builds, the effect will be to switch investment income from his hands to hers for tax purposes.

Over a period of 10 years, starting in 2013, this strategy would shift at least $55,000 in capital from the husband to the wife. Assuming an average annual return of 6 percent, the value of the wife's TFSA at the end of that time will be $76,844 and the plan will be generating more than $4600 a year in tax-free returns.

The greatest beneficiaries will be young people because the longer the time frame, the more investment income is earned in the plan and the greater the tax savings.

Let's consider the case of a couple who are both 30 years old and who adopt twin girls. They decide that the husband will be a stay-at-home dad while the wife remains in her well-paying job as a human resources vice-president for a medium-sized oil company where she earns $150,000 annually.

In order to move some income into his hands, she gives her husband $5500 a year to invest in a TFSA and puts the same amount into her personal plan. He is quite knowledgeable about investing and succeeds in generating an average annual return of 8 percent over the years.

Over 30 years, she shifts a total of $165,000 to him which is invested tax-free. Thanks to his stock market acumen, that grows to a value of $672,902 at the end of that time. He has earned $507,902 that, without TFSAs and the wife's ability to give him the money, would have been taxable in her hands.

Assuming her income stays constant and tax rates don't change (which of course they will, but this is an illustration), the amount of tax saved over 30 years will be somewhere in the vicinity of $200,000 to $250,000, depending on the province of residence.

If she makes the same contributions to her own TFSA and achieves similar returns, their combined tax savings after 30 years will be close to $500,000!

Of course, this couple's financial position would be even better if full income splitting were allowed. But for now, this is a pretty good start.

ACTION SUMMARY

1. Use TFSAs to split investment income between you and your spouse, potentially saving you thousands of tax dollars over the years.

2. Get your spouse to open a plan as well, to double the tax-saving potential.

10
Passing On

I receive dozens of emails each year from older people asking about how they can leave more money to their children and grandchildren when they pass on.

There are ways to achieve this, but they typically involve complex legal structures, such as trusts, and they can be costly. Unless there is a great deal of money involved, it may not be worth the time and expense.

In some ways, Canadians are better off than our neighbours to the south when it comes to passing on assets to the next generation. The United States imposes hefty succession taxes on its well-to-do citizens. The exemption level for such taxes was raised to US$5 million under the administration of George W. Bush, but that higher exemption is to disappear in 2013 unless Congress extends it. That had not happened as of the time of writing.

We have no estate tax as such in Canada. However, our governments have figured out other ways to grab a large chunk of your money when you die that can be almost as onerous.

This happens when the wealth transfer is to the next generation. Your assets can pass to your spouse or common-law partner after your death with no tax implications. The big hit occurs when the last surviving spouse or partner dies and the estate is transferred to the children or other heirs. For most families, the tax bite at this stage occurs in two ways.

Crystallizing of capital gains at death. When you die, all your investments are deemed to have been sold at fair market value. This means that any profits you have on stocks, mutual funds, real property (other than the principal residence), bonds, and so forth are treated as taxable capital gains on your final tax return. (Yes, the government requires that you, or more precisely your estate, file a tax return even after you are dead.)

Closing of all registered plans. Any registered retirement plans (RRSPs, RRIFs, LIFs) that you own are considered to have been terminated on the day you die. All the money in the accounts is treated as personal income on your final tax return.

This can result in a huge tax bill because all the extra income in registered retirement accounts will attract the top marginal rate, which can be as high as 50 percent (Nova Scotia has the top rate). TFSAs are not subject to this tax risk.

The following table shows how much tax could be assessed on a final return depending on where in Canada the deceased lived and on the taxable value of the registered retirement accounts in the estate. It assumes that the assets are taxed at the average rate that applies for the specific income category. However, the total due could be higher if there is other significant income in the year the person passes

Potential Taxes on Registered Retirement Accounts

Value of Plan Assets

Domicile	$100,000	$250,000	$500,000	$750,000	$1,000,000
British Columbia	$25,114	$89,615	$198,865	$308,115	$417,365
Alberta	$26,242	$83,770	$181,270	$278,770	$376,270
Saskatchewan	$28,485	$93,109	$203,109	$313,109	$423,109
Manitoba	$30,718	$99,346	$215,346	$331,346	$447,346
Ontario	$26,912	$95,555	$211,579	$331,503	$451,427
Quebec	$32,008	$103,519	$224,056	$344,594	$465,131
New Brunswick	$28,158	$91,676	$199,926	$308,146	$416,426
Nova Scotia	$31,112	$103,390	$228,390	$353,390	$478,390
Prince Edward Island	$30,811	$100,894	$219,319	$337,744	$456,169
Newfoundland and Labrador	$28,457	$90,935	$196,685	$302,435	$408,185
Northwest Territories	$25,557	$88,683	$196,308	$303,399	$411,558
Yukon	$26,120	$88,296	$194,291	$300,286	$406,281
Nunavut	$23,631	$82,599	$183,849	$285,099	$386,349

that would drive up the total taxable income. Keep in mind that there is no tax on the assets of an RRSP, RRIF, and so on that pass to a surviving spouse.

The figures are based on 2012 rates and do not make provision for special tax treatment, such as the 50-percent capital gains inclusion rate. They are provided by the Ernst & Young online personal tax calculator.[1] They do not include provincial probate fees.

One thing this table tells us is that the best way to minimize tax on the registered assets in your estate is to be a resident of Alberta or Nunavut when you die. Try to avoid dying in Quebec or Nova Scotia, both of which really sock it to the dearly departed.

Even on a relatively modest $100,000 RRIF (taxable income), the heirs of a deceased Quebecer will inherit $8647 less than those of someone who dies in Nunavut. On large estates, the tax gap becomes tens of thousands of dollars. The heirs of a Nova Scotia resident with a million-dollar RRIF will end up with $102,120 less than the survivors of a person who passes away in Alberta leaving behind the same amount. So anyone from the East Coast who left home to work in the oil fields won't do his family any favours by going back to Nova Scotia to die.

TFSAs and Estate Planning

The creation of TFSAs changes the estate-planning ground rules. That's because money accumulated in these plans does not attract any tax at death. Therefore, one of the first priorities of older people who want to maximize the after-tax value of their estates should be to move as much money as possible from non-registered investment accounts into TFSAs.

For example, let's assume two spouses who are both 70 years old have $70,000 invested in non-registered accounts. Of this, $40,000 is in the wife's name and is invested in blue-chip stocks. The husband has the other $30,000 invested in GICs. They have two children to whom they want to leave equal shares of the estate. Neither spouse has opened a TFSA yet.

Looking at this situation strictly from an estate-planning perspective, the GICs will attract little tax at death, since they have no capital gains potential. Only the interest earned will be taxed. The stocks are another matter. The wife's portfolio took a beating in the market collapse of 2008–2009, but she's now back to more or less break-even and she expects the stocks to move back into profit territory as the economy recovers. How should they proceed?

First, they should both open TFSAs immediately. They each have $20,000 in contribution room covering the four years from 2009 to 2012 plus another $5500 for 2013 for a total of $25,500 individually or $51,000 combined.

Next, the wife should transfer $25,500 worth of her stocks into a self-directed TFSA (a contribution in kind). Such a transfer is a deemed sale as far as the Canada Revenue Agency is concerned; if the stocks are all trading at around the same price she originally paid, there will be little or no capital gains tax to pay. Note, however, that she should not contribute any losing stocks directly to a TFSA as the loss will not be allowed for tax purposes. Instead, she should sell the stocks rather than transferring them. By doing so, she crystallizes a capital loss that can be deducted from past, current, or future capital gains.

(Warning: Do not sell losing stocks in a non-registered account and buy them back immediately inside a TFSA. That would trigger what is technically known as the "superficial loss rule," meaning the Canada Revenue Agency would not recognize your capital loss for tax purposes. You must wait 30 days before repurchasing the same stock. However, you can buy shares in a different company any time.)

As for the husband, he can transfer $25,500 worth of his GICs into his own TFSA. The GICs do not have to be sold first; they also can go into the TFSA directly as a contribution in kind.

The couple should continue this process each year until all of the assets have been moved into the TFSAs.

If they begin the process in 2013, they'll be left in this situation: $51,000 of their non-registered assets will have been moved into TFSAs. The wife will still have $14,500 in her non-registered account while the husband will own $4500 in non-registered GICs.

The balance of the GICs can be tax-sheltered in 2014, using the annual contribution room. The rest of the wife's account can be moved into TFSAs by 2016. At this point, the couple's entire non-registered portfolio will have been moved into TFSAs and will be safe from taxation when they die.

RRSP/RRIF Strategies

A similar strategy could be considered with RRSPs and RRIFs, although the fact that any money withdrawn from these plans is taxable immediately makes the decision more complicated. In this situation, the current tax status of the plan holder is a major factor. If the person is in a low tax bracket, taking out an after-tax amount of $5500 a year and moving it into a TFSA may reduce the total tax bite on those savings at death.

Let's look at the case of a B.C. man who is 70 years old and has $100,000 in a RRIF. He is a widower and plans to leave his estate to his only daughter. His annual taxable income is $32,000, which means his marginal tax rate is 20.06 percent (2012 rates). If he were to die at the end of this year, the $100,000 in the RRIF would be added to his income, increasing the total to $132,000 for purposes of his final tax return. The extra tax on the RRIF money would add $33,840 to the assessment, a tax rate of 33.84 percent. So his daughter would inherit only $66,160 of the proceeds of the RRIF after tax.

If the father withdraws an extra $7000 from his RRIF this year, he will be assessed $1457 tax on the payment (an effective rate of 20.81 percent), leaving him with just over $5500 after tax. He can then open a TFSA and deposit $5500 of that, repeating the same process each year. Essentially, he is paying tax at a much lower rate now than would be assessed on the RRIF if he dies. After the money goes into the TFSA, it grows tax-free, and no tax will be assessed on the plan's value at the time of his death.

This strategy is not a guaranteed financial winner because if the father lives long enough, the value of the RRIF may be reduced to the point where the tax assessed at death will be very low anyway. Moreover, by paying tax on the extra withdrawals early, he loses the investment income that this tax money could have earned if it had remained in the RRIF. Over five years, assuming annual compounding of 6 percent, $1457 will generate almost $500 in investment income.

Although it does not apply in this illustration, people 65 or older with higher income need to consider whether extra RRIF or RRSP withdrawals will push them over the Old Age Security clawback threshold, thereby raising their effective tax rate. That would change the entire equation.

You will need to carefully analyze your particular situation before you take any action. If there is a large amount of money involved, consult a financial professional before embarking on this strategy.

Mass Confusion

TFSA succession planning has turned out to be something of a minefield. The reason: divided federal and provincial jurisdictions that resulted in unnecessary confusion and frustration for many account holders in the first six months after the plans were launched in 2009 and are still the source of legal debates over the precise meaning of certain terms.

It all started when Ottawa announced that as part of the TFSA program, anyone opening a plan could designate his or her spouse/partner as the "successor account holder."

Successor holders would receive all the assets in the TFSA if the plan holder died. As a result, successors could withdraw the money tax-free or continue to manage the plan if they wished.

The problem is that succession laws are a provincial responsibility. Ottawa can say what it likes on the matter, but nothing actually happens in the real world until the provinces (and the territories) take action.

In most parts of Canada, that had not happened by the time TFSAs were launched at the beginning of 2009. Only a handful of provinces had passed legislation to allow successor holders to be named (and not by that specific term). The rest dragged their heels, in some cases until mid-year.

There was no excuse for this delay; in most cases, the provinces simply added Tax-Free Savings Accounts to the list of registered plans that were permitted to transfer assets outside of probate.

(Quebec, which has a different set of laws under the Civil Code, never took action to allow for successor holders and never will; residents of that province must name a beneficiary in their will.)

The result was widespread uncertainty when the plans were launched. Residents of some provinces were allowed to make successor holder designations as part of their TFSA application. But in most regions, including populous Ontario, they were not. Since I had urged readers to name a successor account holder in the first edition of this book, I received numerous emails from unhappy people saying that their bank would not allow this and asking what to do.

Mea culpa. The first edition was written in September 2008, and at the time I assumed, incorrectly as it turned out, that the provinces would be onside by the time TFSAs were available. After all, they had been given almost a year's notice. As it turned out, only British Columbia, Alberta, Nova Scotia, New Brunswick, and Prince Edward Island were ready to go. The rest slowly signed on in the months that followed. Ontario was the last of the stragglers, implementing its succession law changes on June 16, 2009, five days after Manitoba. Now that the process is complete, every couple in Canada (outside Quebec) can name a successor holder and probate fees should not apply to TFSA transfers on death, although the provinces can make their own rules in this regard.

The practical effect of this provincial tardiness is that anyone who was unable to name a successor holder when they opened an account must now go back to the plan administrator and complete the required form. I strongly advise doing this, as it will make the whole transfer process much easier if anything should happen to you. Anyone opening a new account should be able to do this without difficulty.

That said, there is still some confusion about the difference between a successor account holder and a beneficiary. You need to understand the distinction because you may have both a successor holder form and a beneficiary form handed to you when you open an account.

To be clear, a successor holder can only be the spouse or common-law partner of the person who owns the TFSA. (Common-law partners must have lived together for at least three years or have children together.) No one else qualifies. The successor holder will take control of the TFSA when the original account holder dies, which means he or she can manage the assets in the plan and may make new contributions after an exemption period once it is transferred to his or her name. However, successor holders do not inherit any unused contribution room from the deceased. Any new contributions will be deducted from their personal limit. The successor holder can also make a new beneficiary designation and may cash out the plan at any time, tax-free.

A beneficiary is anyone else who is named to inherit a plan's assets: a child, sibling, relative, friend, or charity. A beneficiary will receive the assets of a TFSA, tax-free, at death, and the plan will be terminated. However, any profits earned within the TFSA between the time the holder dies and the date it is wound up will be taxable in the hands of the beneficiary.

Tax experts warn not to name your spouse/partner as a beneficiary but rather to use the successor holder designation. If you make a mistake and name the spouse as a beneficiary, the CRA will probably interpret that as meaning successor holder, but why risk complicating matters?

Don't name your spouse and someone else as joint beneficiaries. If you do, the rules of the game change and the transfer of assets will become more complicated because the spouse will no longer qualify as a successor holder.

In general, the rules governing the tax treatment of TFSAs after death are similar to those for RRSPs. TFSAs will retain their tax-exempt status until the end of the year following the year of the plan holder's death. So if a TFSA investor dies during 2013, the plan will keep its tax-exempt status until December 31, 2014. After that, it loses its TFSA status and becomes a plain, non-registered investment account. If that happens, every security in the portfolio will be assigned a fair market value, and any interest, dividends, or capital gains earned after that will be taxed at normal rates.

Let's consider some of the scenarios that can arise on the death of a TFSA plan holder:

1. *The spouse or partner is named as the successor holder.* In this case, the deceased person's TFSA can be continued, combined with the survivor's own TFSA, or the assets can be withdrawn tax-free. The survivor retains his or her own TFSA and the contribution room he or she previously had. In effect, the successor holder simply steps into the shoes of the deceased.

2. *The last surviving spouse or partner dies and the TFSA assets are divided between two children, an adult brother and sister.* In this case, the money in the plan at the time of death remains tax-free. However, any profits earned after death are taxable as income in the children's hands.

   But here is an angle that will likely become increasingly important in estate planning. The executor has the flexibility to decide how the TFSA assets are divided and can use that discretion to minimize the tax due.

Let's assume that the TFSA had $100,000 in assets at the time of the plan holder's death and generated another $20,000 in gains before the estate was settled. In this case, the brother is unemployed and therefore has very little income. The sister is a vice-president of a large company and is in the top tax bracket. As the legislation is currently worded, the executor can direct that the sister's share of the $120,000 in the TFSA be received as a $60,000 tax-exempt transfer. The brother receives $40,000 in tax-exempt money and $20,000 in taxable income. Since he is in a very low bracket, the amount of tax he will actually end up paying will be minimal. (This is a loophole that may be closed in the future, so estate planners will need to keep watch on the situation.)

3. *The status of the TFSA is not resolved by the end of the year following death*. This will be a rare occurrence, but if it happens, the rules state that the TFSA becomes a taxable trust. The money that was in the plan at the time of death retains tax-exempt status. Any gains earned in the plan after death become taxable at trust rates. This status will continue until such time as the trust is liquidated.

4. *The TFSA is left to a charity*. When this is done, the transfer of funds must generally occur within three years of the plan holder's death. Once the donation has been completed, it is possible to ask to have the deceased's tax return for the year of death

adjusted in order to claim the charitable donation tax credit.

You can find more information on the death of a TFSA holder at the Canada Revenue Agency website.[2]

ACTION SUMMARY

1. Move assets from non-registered accounts into TFSAs to reduce tax at death.
2. When transferring securities from non-registered accounts to TFSAs, begin with securities that are likely to appreciate most in value.
3. Consult a financial professional before deciding whether to make early withdrawals from an RRSP or RRIF in order to make TFSA contributions.
4. Unless you live in Quebec, name your spouse or partner as the successor holder when you open a TFSA. There is no standardized form for setting up a TFSA so be sure to review the application carefully. Make sure that it allows you to designate a successor holder. If it does not, ask if there is a separate form for this purpose.
5. Quebec residents should designate the person who is to receive the TFSA assets in their wills.
6. When TFSA assets pass to the next generation, the executor of the estate should ensure they are distributed in the most tax-efficient manner.

11
Tax-Saving Strategies

As we have already seen, there are many ways to save taxes by using TFSAs. However, we have only scratched the surface. Astute accountants and financial planners are continually coming up with more ideas, although some may be complex.

In this chapter, let's look at some easy-to-implement tax-saving strategies that we have not yet examined in depth.

Choose the Right Securities

In order to maximize the tax efficiency of your TFSA, it is essential you choose the right securities for the plan. If you're earning a return of only 0.5 percent, which is what Canada Savings Bonds were paying in the fall of 2012, it's hardly worth the effort to open a plan.

With RRSPs, the conventional wisdom is to hold interest-paying securities, such as bonds and GICs, inside the registered plan while keeping dividend-paying investments and growth stocks in a non-registered account. The logic for this is simple. All income drawn from an RRSP (or a RRIF/LIF) is taxed at your marginal rate, regardless of its original source. This means that interest, dividends, capital gains, and even return of capital are all taxed exactly the same when the money is earned inside a registered plan.

In the real world of non-registered accounts, the tax treatment is much different. Dividends are eligible for the dividend tax credit, which dramatically cuts the rate you actually pay. For example, a Saskatchewan resident with taxable income of $45,000 pays a marginal rate of 35 percent on RRSP or RRIF withdrawals. But the tax rate on dividends from public companies received in a non-registered account is only 12.39 percent. Clearly, it makes sense in this particular case to keep those dividend-paying stocks outside an RRSP if at all possible.

The same is true of any investments that have been purchased with a view to generating capital gains, such as stocks and equity mutual funds. If these securities are held in a non-registered account, only 50 percent of any gain is taxable in most circumstances, and gains can be offset by capital losses. But all capital gains earned in RRSPs and RRIFs will be taxed at your marginal rate when they come out and, to make matters worse, you can't claim any capital losses.

Certain types of securities also produce what is known as return of capital (ROC), which is not taxable in the year it is received. Income that is deemed to be ROC is deducted from the price you originally paid for the security, creating what is called an adjusted cost base (ACB). The ACB is eventually used to calculate any capital gain or loss when the security is sold. The net effect is that you benefit from tax sheltering until you sell, at which time you are taxed at the capital gains rate.[1]

A number of mutual fund companies offer products that make some or all of their distributions in the form of return of capital. But if you hold these inside an RRSP, all this clever tax-saving manipulation is lost.

TFSAs require a change in thinking. Since no taxes are assessed when money comes out of the plan, the RRSP tax planning strategies don't apply. You need to take a different approach if you are going to maximize the tax-free effectiveness of a TFSA.

A Capital Gains Strategy

In their 2006 campaign platform, the federal Conservatives promised to exempt capital gains from tax if the proceeds were reinvested within six months. They never delivered on that pledge, but TFSAs could have the long-term effect of making most capital gains tax-free. (There will be exceptions, such as a vacation property, since direct ownership of real estate within these plans is not permitted.)

So while it is true that capital gains receive a good break when they are earned outside a registered plan, they get even better treatment within a TFSA. Instead of paying tax on half of your profits, you get to keep the whole amount. The only downside is that you can't deduct capital losses incurred within a TFSA against gains made outside a plan.

Focusing a TFSA on capital gains looks even more attractive when we take another look at the contribution rules. Remember that any withdrawals from a plan are added back to your contribution limit in future years. So if you are smart or lucky (or both), you may be able to build your TFSA much faster than you might expect.

Let's consider a scenario that, while hypothetical, is certainly feasible. In the fall and winter of 2008–2009, world stock markets crashed. The S&P/TSX Composite Index lost more than 50 percent from its all-time high in early June 2008 to its low point in March 2009. It then shifted gears and staged a dramatic comeback, gaining more than 52 percent from March to December. This is not unusual; we have seen similar patterns many times before.

The high-tech collapse that opened this century provides a good example. Between the late winter of 2000 and October 2002, stock markets dived, led down by NASDAQ, which eventually lost about 80 percent of its value. But after a final huge sell-off in September and October 2002 (technically known as the "capitulation" stage in a market collapse), a rally began. Between December 31, 2002, and June 6, 2008, the S&P/TSX Composite Index rose from 8221 to 15,155—a gain of 84 percent. Many blue-chip stocks doubled, tripled, even quadrupled in value during that period. At one point during the 2002 sell-off, you could have bought shares in TD Bank for as low as $25.17. In November 2007, you could have sold them for as much as $75, a profit of almost 200 percent.

Resource stocks fared even better. The shares of Potash Corporation of Saskatchewan traded as low as $13.23 during 2002. In June 2008, they touched a high of $246.29—an astounding gain of more than 1700 percent!

The same thing happened after the crash of 2008–2009. You could have bought shares of Bank of Montreal for as little as $25.50 in February 2009, at which time the stock was offering a dividend yield of more than 11 percent. By mid-April 2010, the stock was trading near $65, a gain of more than 150 percent.

Shares of mining giant Teck Resources were going for as low as $3.35 in March 2009. Less than two years later, in January 2011, they were trading at just below $62. They had moved up by almost 1750 percent!

It's unrealistic to expect to pick winners of that magnitude on a consistent basis. What is not unrealistic is the possibility—indeed the probability—that high-quality stocks will double in value in the two to three years following the end of a deep bear market.

Here is a capital gains strategy that flows from that thinking. If you have not already done so, open a TFSA now and invest the $5500 yearly contribution limit plus any carry-forward room you have accumulated in two or three quality stocks. Choose companies that are industry leaders, have a well-established history of surviving even the toughest times, and are trading at the low end of their normal range.

Let's assume you invest a total of $25,500 at the beginning of 2013. You select the stocks carefully and buy when prices are relatively cheap. If the scenario plays out as predicted, after two full years (the end of 2014), your TFSA stands a good chance of showing an increase of 25 percent or more. Using the 25 percent figure, you would now have $31,875 in the plan, assuming no additional contributions.

You decide to sell the stocks and withdraw the cash to

use for the down payment on a rental property. There are no capital gains taxes to pay.

In the next year, your contribution room will be $42,875—the $5500 basic entitlement for 2014 and 2015 plus the $31,875 you withdrew. Now you can begin the process of rebuilding the TFSA to the extent that your financial resources permit. The net result is that you now own an income property plus you have increased the amount of money you can shelter from tax in the future.

Of course, the timing has to be right, you must have the temperament to accept stock market risk, and you must choose the right companies for this to work. But it is a strategy worth considering, especially coming out of a bear market.

A Dividend Strategy

At first glance, it would seem that the capital gains strategy I have described would also apply to dividends. Yes, they get a tax advantage in a non-registered account, but you pay no tax at all if they are earned in a TFSA.

But here's the wrinkle. If your taxable income is relatively low and you invest in dividend stocks with little or no growth potential (preferred shares are a classic example), you may decide to use the TFSA for something else.

There are some quirks to the dividend tax credit that require close examination before you make a decision. Let's look at the situation of a 75-year-old widowed grandmother who lives with her children in Ontario. She has a small pension, which, when added to her CPP and OAS payments, gives her taxable income of $25,000 a year. She has recently inherited a modest investment portfolio from her husband, which consists almost entirely of bank preferred shares. The dividends from the portfolio will add $3000 a year to her income.

In this case, there is no tax advantage to putting the preferred shares into a TFSA (assuming they will never generate a capital gain). That's because, at her income level, the effect of the dividend tax credit will be to reduce the tax payable on the investment income to zero. (This would also be the case in every province except Quebec, Manitoba, and New Brunswick, and in the latter case the tax rate would be only 0.14 percent.)

Compare her situation with that of a Quebec-based senior vice-president of a large public corporation who owns 100,000 shares of the company's common stock and has taxable income of $85,000. In his case, the dividends will be taxed at a rate of 24.74 percent (2012 rates). He should contribute $5500 worth of his shares to a TFSA every year and give his wife $5500 worth to do the same.

There is also another circumstance in which dividend-paying securities should be considered for TFSA accounts. That's when a taxpayer is vulnerable to the Old Age Security clawback. I'll explain this in more detail later in this chapter.

An Interest Strategy

Although interest income is taxed at your marginal rate, the tax-saving potential of a TFSA for GICs, Canada Premium Bonds (CSBs), and so forth is limited, especially at a time when rates are low. For example, if you invested $5000 in the issue of Canada Premium Bonds that came out in November 2012, the total amount of tax-sheltered income you will receive over the first three years will be only $181. That's only about $60 a year! With returns like that, it's hardly worthwhile to set up a plan.

Still, many people prefer the safety of interest-bearing securities to the risk of stock market investing. For those who have a long time horizon, there is certainly an advantage in using a TFSA for this purpose instead of leaving the money in a taxable account. The key is to aim for the highest possible return, consistent with safety.

In the late summer of 2012, for example, a few financial institutions were offering five-year GICs with a yield of 3.25 percent. If you had invested $5000 and tax-sheltered the interest in a TFSA, you would have earned $867 in tax-free profit at maturity.

The obvious moral of this story is if you want to use interest-bearing securities in your TFSA, shop around for the best possible rate.

Avoiding the Dreaded Clawback

One of the most contentious tax laws on the books is the clawback of Old Age Security payments from those Canadians age 65 and older who are deemed to be in the "high-income" category. For the 2012 tax year, the threshold that pushed people into this class was net income exceeding $69,562 (the figure increases annually in line with inflation).

The tax is a stiff one: a 15-percent surcharge on every dollar of net income above the limit until the entire OAS payment has been recovered. For a Manitoba resident with taxable income of $75,000, the effect is to increase the marginal tax rate on the affected portion of her income to 54.4 percent.

Obviously, OAS recipients who are close to the threshold are motivated to do anything they can to stay below it. TFSAs provide two new ways to achieve this.

The first derives from the fact that TFSA withdrawals are not considered to be taxable income, unlike RRSP withdrawals or RRIF payments. This wasn't a significant factor when TFSAs were first launched because of the low $5000 contribution limit. But as of 2013, everyone who was 18 or older when TFSAs became available will have $25,500 in accumulated contribution room. And as time goes on, TFSA balances will continue to increase. This means that people who are close to the threshold will be able to draw cash from the plans without risking having their OAS payments clawed back.

The second way in which TFSAs can be used to reduce or eliminate exposure to the clawback is more subtle. It involves using the plans to circumvent what I regard as one of the most unfair aspects of the Income Tax Act, but one that no government seems willing to change.

We have already looked at the advantages of the dividend tax credit. But the credit can be a double-edged sword when it comes to the OAS clawback. That is because of the way it is calculated and the structure of the income tax return.

There is nothing simple about the dividend tax credit.

Calculating it is a two-stage operation. The first involves a "gross-up" of the actual dividend income you receive to what is technically called the "taxable amount of dividends." The second step is to multiply that number by a percentage factor to arrive at the actual amount you can deduct from your income tax.

For what the government classifies as "eligible dividends," which includes all public companies, that factor is 15 percent. For dividends that are not deemed eligible (typically those from private companies), the factor is 13.3333 percent.[2] As I said, this is not simple!

Here is the problem as it relates to the clawback. The grossed-up amount of dividends received is used to calculate net income. (This is unlike the treatment accorded to capital gains, where only half the profit is included in the net income calculation.) The result is that people who receive dividends run the risk of incurring tax on money that they never actually received—I call it "phantom income."

It works like this. Every dollar of eligible dividend income you collect is grossed up by 38 percent. So, for purposes of calculating exposure to the OAS clawback, $1.00 of income is treated as if you had actually received $1.38. Clearly, people who depend on dividends for a significant portion of their retirement income could find themselves pushed over the clawback threshold as a result.

This is not a theoretical exercise. Low interest rates and the demise of income trusts have forced many older people to look for other investments that will provide them with the cash flow they need to live on. As a result, a lot of people have put money into preferred shares that in some cases offer yields of between 4 percent and 6 percent, depending on the quality of the company.

The trap is the gross-up. Someone who receives $15,000 in eligible dividends in 2013 will have to declare $20,700 as net income, which could be enough to move her into clawback territory.

You can use TFSAs to alleviate this dilemma. By investing in preferred shares (or dividend-paying common stocks), you'll lose the dividend tax credit, but you will also avoid the gross-up problem. This strategy isn't applicable to everyone, but it should be considered by those who have invested (or want to invest) in dividend-paying securities and who have income that brings them close to the OAS threshold.

Inheritance Shelters

The next 10 to 20 years will see an intergenerational transfer of billions of dollars in personal wealth. As the money passes from parents to children, the issue will be how to manage the transfer in a tax-effective way.

As explained in Chapter 10, the money in a TFSA at the time of the death of the last surviving spouse will pass to the next generation tax-free, unlike RRSP/RRIF assets that will be taxed at the decedent's marginal rate. After that, if any portion of the money is invested, the profits are subject to tax at the applicable rates.

So TFSAs offer an efficient way to shelter part or all of an inheritance from future taxes. By 2015, for example, an older couple who has not made any TFSA investments will have $73,000 in available contribution room, as shown in the table in Chapter 3. By 2018, this will have increased to at least $106,000. (It could be more if the Conservatives deliver on their 2011 campaign promise to double the annual TFSA contribution limit once the federal budget is balanced.)

Although this may not be enough to shelter the full amount of an inheritance, it will certainly help to reduce the tax bite when the last spouse dies if they move as much money as possible into TFSAs.

If the couple combines this approach with another tax-avoidance technique, such as paying off any existing mortgage on their tax-free principal residence, the proceeds from all but the largest estates may eventually end up being tax-exempt when the parents pass on.

The same principle applies to lottery winnings, should you be so lucky.

Investment Loans

It's against the law to use an RRSP as collateral for a loan. That is not the case with a TFSA. The money in a TFSA can be used as security if you need to borrow cash for any reason. This loan can be for any purpose, from obtaining emergency funds to adding to your investments.

To illustrate, let's assume that you have accumulated $20,000 in a TFSA and invested the money in five-year GICs. Unless you have chosen redeemable GICs, that cash is locked in until maturity.

Suddenly, you are laid off and you need the money. You can't cash in the GICs, but you can go to the bank and ask them for a loan, using the assets of your TFSA as collateral. Since the money in the plan is in guaranteed certificates, there should be no problem obtaining the temporary cash you need.

Another possibility, and one that will probably be promoted by financial advisers during periods when stock markets are rising, is to use the money in a TFSA to leverage your investment portfolio. Because of the risks involved, this is not a strategy I recommend except for very knowledgeable investors, but if you know what you are doing, it is a way to potentially increase profits. (It's also a way to increase losses, as people who had borrowed to invest learned to their dismay in the crash of 2008–2009.)

To illustrate this situation, let's look five years down the road. You've been contributing the maximum amount to a TFSA every year and, with the earnings on the invested money, your plan has a value of $75,000. The entire amount is held in a diversified portfolio of mutual funds.

You decide to use the TFSA as collateral to borrow additional money to invest. Since the mutual funds are not guaranteed, the bank won't offer a loan equal to the full value of the plan, but it agrees to advance you $50,000 at prime plus 1 percent—we'll say 4 percent for purposes of this example. You invest the money in a non-registered portfolio of mutual funds, bringing the total amount of your assets to $125,000, of which $75,000 is in the TFSA and $50,000 in the new portfolio. You invest the borrowed money in dividend-paying stocks.

Over the next five years, your non-registered investments earn an average of 8 percent annually. At the end of that time, the original $50,000 will have increased to $73,466. Assuming an average tax rate of 20 percent on the non-registered portfolio (your profits came mainly from dividends and capital gains), the $50,000 you invested there will be worth $68,773 after tax for a profit of $18,773.

However, you need to subtract the interest cost of the loan from your return. And here's where an interesting tax twist comes into play. As is the case with RRSP loans, you cannot deduct the interest expense on money borrowing to invest *in* a TFSA. But you can deduct interest on a loan *against* a TFSA if the money is used to invest in a non-registered portfolio, say Gena Katz of Ernst & Young Canada and Jamie Golombek of CIBC Private Wealth Management. This means that a portion of the annual $2000 interest on this loan can be written off. Assuming a marginal tax rate of 40 percent, that would reduce the net annual cost of carrying the loan to $1200, or $6000 over the five years. So your actual gain on the borrowed $50,000 after five years is $12,773.

At this point, you repay the bank loan and pocket the money. The end result is that you have completed the transaction with a net return of 25.5 percent on the money you borrowed. Whether that's enough to warrant the risk you took by leveraging is for you to decide. The point is that the option is available, if you choose to use it.

ACTION SUMMARY

1. Give careful thought to the securities you hold in your TFSA, with a view to maximizing tax effectiveness.

2. Be sure you understand the differences between the tax-planning guidelines for RRSPs and RRIFs and those for TFSAs.

3. Focusing a TFSA on capital gains has the potential of producing large profits quickly, especially coming out of a bear market. Beware of the increased risk in this approach.

4. Do not automatically invest in dividend-paying stocks within a TFSA, especially those with little or no capital gains potential, such as preferred shares. This is especially important for lower-income people. Examine the tax implications carefully before deciding.

5. If you use a TFSA to hold interest-bearing securities such as bonds or GICs, look for the highest return consistent with safety.

6. The "gross-up" applied to dividends can result in some people who collect Old Age Security being pushed into an extremely high tax bracket on the basis of money they never actually receive. Anyone at risk of being in this position should consider putting dividend-paying stocks in a TFSA.

7. Use TFSAs to shelter intergenerational inheritances from tax.

8. TFSAs can be used as collateral for a loan, and the interest may be tax-deductible if the money is used for investment purposes. If—and only if—you are experienced and knowledgeable, you can take advantage of this to increase the size of your investment portfolio through leveraging.

12

Special Situations

Since the launch of Tax-Free Savings Accounts in January 2009, I have received hundreds of questions from people who were trying to understand the ins and outs of this great investment opportunity.

One came from a woman who asked whether she would earn more profit by moving her money from a U.S. index fund to a TFSA. "I am not really sure which is the better investment," she wrote.

In my reply, I explained that the two were not mutually exclusive. Think of a TFSA as an empty box, I suggested. You can fill it with any kind of investments you want, provided you have the right type of plan and they qualify under the guidelines of the Canada Revenue Agency. So, if she wished to do so, she could open a self-directed TFSA and transfer the U.S. index fund directly into it, up to the contribution limit.

After she received my reply, she wrote back, "Thank you for your response. It appears there is more to this than just dumping $5000 into a TFSA."

Yes, there certainly is, which is why this book was written. The plain fact is that although the plans will be entering their fifth year in 2013, many people still don't understand how to use them effectively. And with each passing year the

complexities surrounding TFSAs become more apparent. In
this chapter, I'll look at some of the special situations that
have emerged thus far.

U.S. Dividends

Several years ago, Canada and the United States reached an
agreement to recognize and respect the integrity of the tax-
sheltered retirement savings plans available in each country.
This understanding was subsequently formalized as part of
the Canada-U.S. Tax Treaty.

Under the terms of the agreement, dividends paid by
American corporations into Canadian retirement plans
such as RRSPs and RRIFs are exempt from the 15 percent
withholding tax that applies to payments made to non-
registered accounts. Americans receive the same treatment
for Canadian dividends paid into IRAs, 401(k) plans, and
so on.

However, TFSAs are not covered by the tax treaty and
may never be, as they are not considered to be "retirement
accounts" because the money can be used for any purpose.
Therefore, the exemption from U.S. withholding tax does not
apply to dividends paid to your TFSA. As a result, your plan
will receive only 85 percent of any dividend declared by an
American company whose stock you own.

That's not the only financial penalty for putting
U.S. stocks into a TFSA. In the case of non-registered
accounts, investors can recover part or all of the 15 percent
withholding tax by claiming a foreign tax credit when they

file their Canadian returns. That credit is not available when the dividend is paid to a TFSA because the income is tax-sheltered. The bottom line is that the investor is out of luck as far as the tax people are concerned.

This creates a disincentive for holding U.S. dividend-paying stocks in a TFSA. However, don't write them off entirely because there is another way to look at this. If you receive U.S. dividends outside a TFSA, they will be taxed at your marginal rate (non-Canadian dividends are not eligible for the dividend tax credit). That means you could pay tax at a rate as high as 50 percent, depending on where you live and your total income. Inside a TFSA, the dividends will be taxed at only a 15 percent rate—the U.S. withholding tax.

That actually may be a better deal than holding the U.S. shares in an RRSP or RRIF, and that's because withdrawals from those plans are taxed at your marginal rate. So, while you avoid the withholding tax at the time of the payments, you'll be hit when the dividends come out, probably at a higher rate than 15 percent.

So don't automatically exclude U.S. stocks from your TFSA. Just be sure you understand that, in this particular situation, any profits will not be entirely tax-free.

Moving Abroad

Just because Canada recognizes a particular plan as a tax shelter does not mean that another country will. So, if you are considering taking up residence abroad, you need to give some thought to your TFSA and what to do about it.

Only Canadian residents can contribute to a TFSA. But if you already have a plan and move elsewhere, you are allowed to keep it and to make withdrawals from it. As far as Canada is concerned, any such withdrawals will continue to be tax-free. But your new host country may not be so generous.

For example, if you move to the United States, the Internal Revenue Service (IRS) will recognize assets in an RRSP or RRIF at the time you take up residence there as capital and therefore not taxable. Plus any income earned within the plan after you become a U.S. resident may continue to compound tax-free. You only become liable for U.S. taxes once you start making withdrawals and then only on those amounts that relate to income earned in your RRSP or RRIF after you became a U.S. resident, plus any unrealized capital gains.

(This makes it a sound strategy to take any capital gains in your RRSP before you leave Canada, thereby reducing the U.S. tax for which you'll eventually be liable. If you've lost money in your RRSP to the extent that the plan's value is less than your total contributions, you'll face no U.S. tax at all.)

You will have to pay a withholding tax of 25 percent in Canada when you make withdrawals from your RRSP after you become a non-resident by moving to the United States. Periodic payments from a RRIF, LIF, or annuity are subject to a 15-percent withholding tax. (Withholding rates may differ if you move to another country; the standard rate on pensions, RRIFs, and annuities is 25 percent, but any tax treaty provisions take precedence.)

Those are the RRSP/RRIF rules. However, TFSAs don't get such generous treatment. As far as the IRS is concerned, they are simply foreign investment accounts, and any interest, dividends, or capital gains earned in them are taxable. This would apply to American citizens living in Canada who have to file U.S. tax returns as well as to Canadians with TFSAs who become U.S. residents.

"A TFSA has no special status under the Internal Revenue Code and there are no relieving provisions contained in the Canada-United States Tax Convention (1980)," says a report published by the Tax Specialist Group, an association of independent tax consulting firms. "As such, U.S. taxpayers are taxable on any income earned in a TFSA on a current year basis. This taxable status eliminates the TFSA benefits for most Canadian resident U.S. taxpayers. In some cases, U.S. taxpayers with other investment income may have sufficient Canadian taxes that they will be able to shelter the potential U.S. tax on TFSA income with foreign tax credits."[1]

However, in the case of Canadians moving south of the border, any money in the TFSA at the time they take up U.S. residency would be considered as capital and could be withdrawn tax-free, says Gena Katz, executive director, Tax Practice, with the accounting firm of Ernst & Young. "Either they represent pre-resident capital or income that has been taxed in the U.S. and is now capital," she wrote in an email response to a question.

Clearly, you need to tread very carefully if you find yourself in this situation.

There is another potential problem. Canadian brokers who are not registered in the United States (which is most of them) cannot make trades in your account once you become a non-resident. Even those who are registered are limited in what they are allowed to do. State regulations make matters even more complicated. So, before you leave Canada to take up permanent residency elsewhere, make sure you sit down with your financial adviser and discuss exactly what the status of your TFSA will be after you depart in terms of your ability to make trades (ask the same question if you have a RRIF or an RRSP). If the account will be frozen, you may decide to close it before you leave. If there is a lot of money involved, this is a major decision, so explore all the options thoroughly.

Jamie Golombek, managing director, Tax and Estate Planning for CIBC Private Wealth Management, says that the tax advantages of keeping the account after emigrating would mostly be lost since it is unlikely the country you are moving to will recognize the tax-free status of the TFSA. "If you are going to leave Canada permanently, while not necessary, you may wish to cash out the TFSA before you go. If you withdraw the money before you become a resident of another country, you know it won't be taxed (unless you're a U.S. citizen). There is no such assurance once you leave."

Ms. Katz agrees: "Unless there is tax relief, there is no benefit to keeping a TFSA if an individual will become a permanent non-resident."

Wilmot George, director, Tax and Estate Planning at Mackenzie Financial, says there may be some special situations in which keeping the TFSA makes sense: "If a client has U.S. foreign tax credits for tax paid on foreign income, the credits can generally be used to offset U.S. tax on TFSA income even though the credits are not sourced from TFSA income. This is particularly useful if a client plans to return to Canada in the future and would like to leave the TFSA in place."

He also notes that if you keep your TFSA after moving to the United States and the value of the plan exceeds US$10,000, you may need to file an FBAR form (Report of Foreign Banks and Financial Accounts) with the IRS. The form is used to collect information on foreign plans to ensure tax and regulatory compliance.

The bottom line is that in most cases the best course of action is to cash in your TFSA if you plan to move to the U.S. or any other foreign country.

Shares in Small Businesses

One of the fastest ways to build assets in a TFSA is to use a self-directed plan to hold shares of a small business with high growth potential. This is perfectly legal, but the rules are complex, and you must be careful to adhere to them.

I received the following question from a reader who had managed to build the $5000 he contributed to his TFSA early in 2009 to $12,000 by August of that year. Now he wanted to aim even higher. He wrote:

I own shares in a private company (some held in a non-registered account, some in my RRSP). The company will be going public later this year. So I have three questions:

1. *Is it possible to use cash in my TFSA to buy more shares in the private company (assuming I have the opportunity to buy more)?*
2. *If "no" to #1, is it possible to swap the private shares in my non-registered account for cash in my TFSA prior to the company getting publicly listed?*
3. *If "no" to #2, is it possible to swap the private shares in my non-registered account for cash in the TFSA the instant they are publicly listed, and at the share price I paid rather than whatever the market value turns out to be that day or at close of day?*

I've had conflicting information from my current broker, from CRA, and from articles I've read. I hope you can shed some light!

For starters, TFSAs use the same rules for holding small business shares as those that apply to RRSPs. In general, these allow a plan holder to invest in the stock of an active Canadian small business provided the contributor (or a plan beneficiary) is not a "connected shareholder."

(The CRA's definition of a connected shareholder is a person who owns 10 percent or more of the company's stock at the time the shares go into the registered plan unless the person deals at arm's length with the firm and the aggregate cost of all shares owned is not more than $25,000.)

Also, it must be clear that any profit on the stock does not represent a payment to the plan holder by the issuer of the shares.

The small business does not have to be publicly traded. It may be an active taxable Canadian corporation, a venture capital company, or a "specified holding company." However, it must qualify as "Canadian," which means that at least 50 percent of its full-time employees are in Canada or at least 50 percent of the salaries "are reasonably attributable to services provided in Canada."

So let's go back to the reader's questions with these facts in mind.

Yes, he can use the cash in his TFSA to buy shares in the private company, as long as it meets the eligibility tests and he is not a connected shareholder. However, the shares must be purchased at fair market value, which may not be easy to determine if the company does not trade publicly.

No, he cannot swap the private shares in his non-registered account for the cash in the TFSA, either before or after it goes public. Amendments to the Income Tax Act introduced in October 2009 prohibit this kind of transaction.

Obviously, this can be a tricky situation. If there is any doubt at all, I suggest obtaining professional advice before proceeding. The penalties for holding prohibited securities in a TFSA are severe, and swaps are now offside as well. And keep in mind that even though a particular manoeuvre may be legal, not all brokerage firms may be willing to execute it. Each company has its own policies and procedures, so discuss the situation with the broker or a supervisor first.

ACTION SUMMARY

1. Dividends from U.S. companies paid into a TFSA will be subject to a 15-percent withholding tax and there is no way to recover that money. So consider the situation carefully before you buy U.S. stocks for your portfolio.

2. If you plan to emigrate from Canada permanently, give serious consideration to cashing in your TFSA before you leave. In all probability, your new country of residence will not recognize the tax-free status of the plan. That is certainly the case for the U.S.

3. Shares in a small business corporation are eligible for inclusion in a TFSA provided they meet CRA requirements. But they must be contributed or purchased at fair market value and cannot be swapped into a plan. Professional advice is recommended.

13
How to Invest

TFSAs are unlike any government-sanctioned savings plan we've seen before. All the others have a specific purpose: retirement planning, education savings, or building an account for a disabled person. By contrast, a TFSA can be used for anything.

It can be a source of emergency money. It can be used for saving to buy a home. It can be a supplementary retirement plan. It can be used to build a tax-sheltered estate. It can be a speculative investment account. Or it can be all of these at various times.

In short, a TFSA can be whatever you want it to be. You define the objectives and set the time frames. Then you decide how to invest the money so as to achieve your goals most effectively.

Canadians seem to be doing that, at least to some extent. A survey released by CIBC in August 2012 found that 36 percent of the respondents who had a plan said they were using it to save for retirement. The creation of an emergency fund was the goal of 30 percent of those with a plan, while 17 percent said they intended to use the money for a major purchase such as a house or car.

But an amazing 41 percent said they had no idea what

they will do with the money. They just wanted to avoid paying taxes.

The fluid nature of a TFSA makes it impossible to establish specific investment guidelines that will be suitable to all plans. There are no "right" or "wrong" investments; it all depends on what you are trying to achieve. For example, someone looking to maximize capital gains within a plan would never even consider investing in a money market fund. But for someone who wants a virtually risk-free source of ready cash to use in an emergency, a money fund may be a perfect fit.

This puts the onus on TFSA investors to choose the right type of plan and to think out their investment strategies very carefully before making decisions. If you don't know how you intend to use the money, it's impossible to develop a suitable investment strategy.

One thing you absolutely should not do is to walk into a financial institution and tell the person behind the counter that you want to open a TFSA without specifying which type. You could end up with a plan that is totally unsuited to your needs. Decide in advance what your primary investment goal will be and then select the type of plan that best suits your objective. Once that is done, choose investments that fit the strategy.

If your main goal is to build an emergency fund, see Chapter 5, "Rainy Day TFSAs," for suggestions on where to invest. Here are some ideas if you have different priorities.

Saving for a Home

As I pointed out in Chapter 6, your first choice if you are saving money to buy a home should be an RRSP. You can build your assets much more quickly because RRSPs have higher contribution limits than TFSAs. Once you have accumulated $25,000, you can borrow the money interest-free to use for a down payment on a house under the provisions of the popular Home Buyers' Plan (HBP).

However, you can use a TFSA to add to your house savings. And if you don't qualify for the HBP because you or your spouse has owned a home within a certain time frame, a TFSA is certainly a worthwhile alternative. (There are some other restrictions to the HBP as well; check the Home Buyers' Plan guide available on the Canada Revenue Agency website.)

If you use a TFSA, there are three important considerations in planning your investment strategy. The first is to decide how much money you want to have available for the down payment. The second is to set a target date for accumulating the money you need. The third is to determine an appropriate risk/reward trade-off.

In most cases, a long-term savings plan is not appropriate. People don't want to wait 20 years for a house. So we'll set the time frame at a maximum of five years.

As for how much you need to save, that's a mathematical calculation. For a conventional mortgage, you'll require at least 20 percent of the cost of the house as a down payment. So, if you are thinking in terms of a $300,000 home, you'll need $60,000. For a two-income couple, let's say that's $30,000 each.

That's the easy part. Deciding on how much risk to accept is more difficult. One of the axioms of investing is the higher the potential return, the greater the risk involved. It's understandable that people want to save enough for a down payment as quickly as possible, but at what cost? Imagine the disappointment if you had been about ready to buy a home in mid-2008 and then saw half your savings wiped out in the market crash.

So let's do some calculations. Suppose you and your spouse/partner are starting to save for a house this year. You each intend to contribute $5500 annually to a TFSA for the next five years. What rate of return do you need to generate to have $30,000 in each plan at the end of that time?

The answer is 2.92 percent. You can't achieve that level of return by holding the money in a savings account. However, you should be able to do so using GICs from smaller financial institutions. That's the low-risk way to proceed.

But you can do better if you are willing to take some risk. A 6-percent average annual return would give you $32,864 after five years. You could use the extra money to help pay for carpets or furniture. A good balanced mutual fund might do the job, providing there are no market meltdowns over the period. Balanced funds are normally relatively low risk, but even the most cautiously managed of them suffered in the 2008–2009 stock market dive.

If you don't like the additional risk, stick with safe GICs and protect yourself from unexpected loss. Just be sure all the GICs will have matured by the time you need the cash.

The type of TFSA chosen will depend on the strategy used.

If the decision is safety first, a GIC plan is a good choice. If you are willing to take more risk to earn a higher return, a mutual fund or self-directed plan is recommended. See Chapter 15 for some suggested portfolios that can be used in this situation.

Maximizing Profits

Many people will see TFSAs as an opportunity to score big tax-free investment gains. If you have a lot of investing experience and can handle the risk, you may be in that group. But keep your priorities straight. Pay off your debts and top up your RRSP before setting out to make a tax-sheltered fortune.

A "big hit" approach requires a self-directed plan that allows you to trade all types of TFSA-eligible securities. Since anyone who goes this route is presumably quite knowledgeable about the markets, a discount brokerage account is preferable because of the reduced costs.

There may be a temptation to focus on speculative penny stocks in your plan, but you can reduce the risk significantly by buying blue chips when they're cheap. For example, investors sold off energy stocks in the fall of 2008 on fears of a global economic collapse. The prices fell so much that you could have bought shares of Suncor Energy in mid-November of that year for $20.62. Less than one year later they were trading at almost $40. Investors who bought at the low almost doubled their money! We saw a similar phenomenon with bank stocks and mining shares, as well as with numerous other companies.

The best strategy in this situation is to buy a quality stock when the price is down and wait until it (hopefully) doubles. At that point take half-profits and buy something else. This will enable you to diversify your TFSA portfolio, thereby reducing risk. You'll find more about this in Chapter 15.

Retirement Savings

If you want to use a TFSA as a retirement savings vehicle to supplement a pension plan and/or an RRSP, you should aim for a respectable rate of growth. However, you must be careful to avoid undue risk.

In this case, consider your TFSA as a personal pension plan. Now think about how professional money managers handle pension accounts. They are very conservative, and with good reason. These men and women have been entrusted with the retirement savings of all the contributors to the plan, who are depending on them to ensure that the money will be there when it comes time to draw on it. So the last thing they can afford is to take big risks that might result in heavy losses. Your TFSA should be handled the same way. Risk should be kept to a minimum and your securities should be chosen accordingly.

Over the years, I have seen a tendency in people to throw caution to the winds in their RRSP accounts and suffer the consequences for their recklessness. I believe there are two reasons for this. One is the fact that retirement seems a long way off, especially to anyone under 40. As a result, the assets in an RRSP take on a sort of Monopoly-money aura. So taking some chances doesn't seem like a big deal. If things don't work out there will be no impact on the person's lifestyle, so why not roll the dice?

There is a danger of the same attitude with some TFSAs. Money will be invested carelessly, with little thought given to the importance of capital preservation. Then another stock market collapse will occur such as we experienced in 2008–2009 and people will be bewailing the losses they have suffered and complaining that they have been forced to put their retirement plans on hold as a result. If you are counting on your TFSA to help you maintain your lifestyle when you stop work, don't make that mistake.

In my book *Retirement's Harsh New Realities*, I recommended that asset allocation within an RRSP be adjusted according to age, making the plan more conservative as the holder approaches retirement. The same formula could be applied to a retirement savings TFSA. Here it is:

Asset Allocation within a Retirement Savings TFSA by Age

	20–25	26–49	50–59	60–65	66+
Cash	5%	5%	10%	10%	15%
Fixed income	30%	20%	30%	40%	50%
Variable income	10%	10%	10%	15%	15%
Growth	55%	65%	50%	35%	20%

Cash includes currency and highly liquid cash-equivalent securities such as treasury bills, money market funds, and Canada Premium Bonds—any asset that can quickly be converted to cash for its full face value qualifies.

Fixed-income securities pay a specified (fixed) rate of return and have a maturity date, at which time your principal is returned. Bonds, mortgages, fixed-rate preferred shares, and GICs fall into this asset class.

Variable-income securities offer cash flow on a predictable basis (usually monthly or quarterly), but the amount of the payment is not guaranteed and may vary considerably. These securities may or may not have a maturity date. Examples include floating-rate preferred shares, income mutual funds, some exchange-traded funds, and income trusts (there are still a few of those left despite the imposition of the new trust tax in 2011).

Growth assets add value mainly through capital gains. Stocks and equity mutual funds are the most common examples.

Looking at the table, you'll see that for the 20 to 25 age group the fixed-income recommendation is higher than for those in the 26 to 49 range while the growth component is smaller. I believe younger people who are just starting out should take a balanced approach to investing until they have learned more about how securities perform and better understand the ins and outs of portfolio management. There is a danger—and I have seen it happen—that young people may tend to be somewhat aggressive with their initial investments. It's a risk I would advise you to avoid if you are serious about using a TFSA as a retirement-savings plan.

As a person becomes more comfortable with investing— and the ages shown here are only a broad guideline—the percentage of higher-risk variable-income and growth securities in the plan can be increased. People in their late twenties, thirties, and even their forties can take a long-term view of the markets and not be overly concerned about temporary setbacks. However, I recommend that a portion of all portfolios be kept in fixed-income securities, both to mitigate risk and to take advantage of those occasions when bonds outperform stocks as they did in Canada for much of the period from mid-2008 to mid-2012.

As you approach your retirement years, you should gradually reduce the risk in your portfolio since the time left to ride out any severe stock market setback is running short. Build your cash and income components, which will be needed when the time comes to convert your savings to a revenue stream. However, I suggest you always retain a portion of your portfolio in growth securities as a protection against even modest rates of inflation. You don't want to outlive your money!

Suitable securities for a retirement savings TFSA include money market funds, bonds, bond funds, GICs, preferred shares, balanced funds, conservatively managed large-cap equity funds, and carefully selected low-risk equities such as utility stocks. Avoid speculative stocks and high-volatility mutual funds and exchange-traded funds (ETFs).

I have developed several age-related retirement savings portfolios based on my asset allocation model, which you will find in Chapter 15.

Education Savings

Although an RESP is the best way to save for a child's education, some parents may wish to avoid the tax risk associated with those plans (see Chapter 8) or use a TFSA to put additional money aside.

If this is your main goal, the key to success is to reduce the investment risk in the plan as the child gets older. By the time he or she is ready to begin post-secondary education, the assets in the plan should be entirely in cash and fixed-income securities so as to ensure that the money for tuition, books, and so on will be available. There is nothing worse than scrimping and saving for years only to see it all wiped out by a stock market bust just as your youngster is ready to start university.

For education savings, I suggest using either a mutual fund plan or a self-directed TFSA. If the child is very young and the initial amount invested is small, begin with a conservatively managed, balanced fund. This will provide immediate diversification while keeping risk to a minimum. As the assets grow, you can add more funds to the account.

Let's assume you begin the process when the child is a baby and that you expect he or she will enter university at age 18. Here is how the asset mix could be adjusted as the child ages. (Note that I have dropped the variable-income line from this table, since it is not as relevant here.)

**Asset Allocation within an Education
Savings TFSA by Child's Age**

	0–10	11–14	15–18	19+
Cash	5%	10%	15%	50%
Fixed income	20%	35%	60%	50%
Growth	75%	55%	25%	0%

The purpose of this approach is to maximize the growth potential of the plan in the early years. After age 10, the risk is reduced by cutting back on the growth weighting. Once the student enters university, all the assets should be in cash and fixed-income securities. This will preserve capital while ensuring that the money will be available to draw on as needed.

As for which securities to select, the same broad rules apply as for retirement savings. See Chapter 15 for more details.

Post-Retirement Income

TFSAs have opened a whole new world of investing opportunities for older people. Until they were introduced, there was no cheap and effective way to tax-shelter investment income after age 71, the year when RRSPs must be terminated. But there is no age limit for contributing to a TFSA, so Canadians who have passed the RRSP cut-off and have some money to invest should take advantage of these plans.

Most people in this age group will have one of two goals. Either they will see a TFSA as a way to provide a tax-sheltered estate for their heirs or they will want to make periodic withdrawals from the plan to supplement their retirement income.

If generating tax-free income is the main objective, focus on low- to medium-risk securities that provide decent cash flow. Examples include high-grade corporate bonds (rated BBB or better), good-quality preferred shares, conservative dividend-paying stocks (for example, utilities), some REITs, and monthly income mutual funds or ETFs. A self-directed TFSA is best suited for this purpose.

If possible, don't make withdrawals from the TFSA for a few years to allow the capital to build to a respectable level. Once you begin drawing income, try to limit the annual amount to no more than the cash flow generated within the plan over the previous 12 months. That way, your capital will remain intact.

Estate Planning

If you are using a TFSA to build a tax-sheltered inheritance for your heirs, you probably want to provide maximum protection for the assets in the plan. At this stage in your life, growth is not the main objective, and presumably you don't need additional income. Rather, you want to preserve the wealth that you have accumulated over the years and ensure that your children or other heirs will benefit from it.

In that case, your TFSA should be as risk-free as possible. An easy way to achieve that is to open a GIC plan and invest all the money in guaranteed investment certificates. GICs are covered by deposit insurance up to $100,000 (or more in some cases). Just be sure the issuing institution is a member of the Canada Deposit Insurance Corporation (CDIC) or is covered by a provincial insurance plan.

A laddered GIC portfolio is the best choice. This involves investing 20 percent of the money in GICs that mature in each of the next five years. This ensures that a portion of the cash is available each year, which may be important for estate settlement purposes after your death. If cash is not needed at the time a GIC matures, the proceeds can be rolled over in a new five-year certificate so as to maximize the interest earned.

Most GICs have a minimum investment requirement of $1000, so the laddered approach will work as long as your TFSA has at least $5000 in it.

ACTION SUMMARY

1. Decide on your priorities before opening a TFSA. The type of plan you choose and the securities you select will be determined in large part by your goals.
2. If you are saving to buy a home, a time frame of no more than five years is recommended. You need to give careful thought to how much risk you will accept.
3. You don't have to invest in penny mining stocks to maximize capital gains. Blue-chip stocks purchased when they're cheap can be surprisingly lucrative.
4. If you use a TFSA for retirement savings, treat it as a personal pension plan.

5. An RESP is the best way to save for a child's education. If you use a TFSA as well, make sure all the assets are in cash or fixed-income securities when the student is ready for college.

6. Older people may wish to use a TFSA to protect their assets for their heirs. GICs are well suited to this purpose.

14
Choosing Your Plan

There are essentially five types of TFSAs and it's important that you choose the right one for your needs. Making a mistake at the outset can end up costing you a lot of money later, in two ways. I'll explain how that can happen in a moment, but first let's look at the five options you need to consider.

Savings Plans

This is likely what you'll end up with if you walk into your local bank or credit union and ask to open a TFSA without specifying which type. Your money will be put into a high-interest savings account, which means it will earn very little income as long as rates remain low. This type of plan is only suitable for those who want to use their TFSA as an emergency fund. Your money is safe (protected by deposit insurance) and is readily available if needed. If an emergency fund is not your primary goal, you need to consider a different option.

GIC Plans

Here your money will be invested in guaranteed investment certificates, usually for a five-year term unless you specify otherwise. There are several types of GICs from which you can choose. The names vary from one financial institution to another but here are the most common types you'll be offered.

Non-redeemable GICs. Your money is locked in until maturity and you receive a guaranteed rate of return, compounded annually or semi-annually. If you need to access the cash sooner, there may be a costly penalty involved. These GICs usually offer the highest interest rate.

Redeemable GICs. These allow you to take your money out before maturity; however, the interest rate you receive will be less.

Interest-linked GICs. These GICs are redeemable. The principal is guaranteed, but the interest rate is variable and is tied directly to another rate, such as prime. However, that does not mean that you will receive the benchmark rate—far from it. For example, in late August 2012, the Royal Bank's prime rate was 3 percent. However, its Prime-Linked Cashable GIC offered only 0.25 percent on deposits between $5000 and $50,000, paid semi-annually or at maturity. Even deposits of more than one million dollars earned only 1 percent.

Market-linked GICs. There is no guaranteed interest rate on most of these certificates. Your return is based on the performance of a benchmark stock index such as the S&P/TSX Composite Index, calculated from the time you make the investment until maturity. But you may only receive a portion of the market's gains—some of these GICs contain clauses setting a cap on how much you can earn. This limits the bank's liability if we have a huge bull market while you own the GIC, but it may leave you wondering why you didn't earn a higher return.

Building block GICs. These enable you to build your GIC by making weekly, biweekly, or monthly deposits to the plan. The interest rate is set at the outset. Maturities are short—in some cases only one year. They are really a form of forced saving.

GICs are useful only for TFSA investors whose top priority is safety of principal and who want a slightly better return than a high-interest savings account offers. Remember that if you choose a locked-in plan, your money will be tied up until maturity.

Mutual Fund Plans

Most financial institutions offer TFSAs that allow you to invest in their own line of mutual funds. In some cases, third-party funds (those from other companies) may also be available. If a mutual fund plan is what you want, look for a TFSA that offers a wide range of choices. There is more risk in this type of TFSA—your money is not protected by deposit insurance, and the value of your investments could decline. The offsetting benefit is much greater profit potential.

Multiple-Option Plans

If you want the greatest flexibility from a bank or credit union TFSA, ask for a multiple-option plan. These enable you to invest in any product offered by the financial institution: savings accounts, GICs, and mutual funds. This allows you to mix and match according to your needs. For example, you could keep a percentage of the TFSA in a savings account for emergency needs and invest the rest in mutual funds for growth.

Self-Directed Plans

You will need to have a broker to open this type of TFSA. It allows you to invest in any type of security that is eligible for a registered plan including stocks, bonds, exchange-traded funds, REITs, and mutual funds. You'll pay more for this flexibility. Some brokers will charge a flat annual fee, while in other cases the amount will be a percentage of the assets in the plan. Make sure that you inquire about the costs up front. Self-directed plans are best suited to knowledgeable investors who are willing to take a higher degree of risk.

The Wrong Plan

Even before Tax-Free Savings Accounts were officially launched in January 2009, people were signing up for them by the tens of thousands. That enthusiasm was great as far as the financial industry was concerned. The problem was that many of those people had no idea what they were doing and ended up with the wrong plan.

That didn't become apparent until the summer of 2010 when it was revealed that the Canada Revenue Agency had sent letters to more than 72,000 TFSA holders advising them that they had overcontributed to their plans during the 2009 tax year and were being assessed penalty interest as a result.

Predictably, that led to an uproar in the media, which ended when the CRA backed down and said that taxpayers who could show the overcontribution was an honest mistake would be given a free pass.

But how could it happen that so many people had made such a mistake? In many cases, it was because they had chosen the wrong type of plan initially and decided to change.

You aren't stuck with the same TFSA for life. You can switch plans or even open several of them. But it has to be done according to the rules.

The mistake that some people made was to close the "wrong" plan—usually a savings account—take the money, and use it to open a new account elsewhere. A typical example would be an individual who invested $5000 in a savings plan in January 2009 and then realized a few months later that self-directed plans were available. He closed the savings TFSA and went to a brokerage firm where he put the $5000 in the type of account he wanted.

As far as the Canada Revenue Agency was concerned, that amounted to a $5000 overcontribution. The taxpayer used up his contribution limit for 2009 when he opened the first

TFSA. By withdrawing the money and reinvesting it elsewhere before the beginning of 2010, he opened himself to penalty interest of 1 percent per month on the $5000, or $50.

He could have avoided that by arranging a direct TFSA-to-TFSA transfer, which is perfectly legal. But he didn't realize that at the time, and a lot of people still don't know this is possible. This is one reason why it is so important to choose the correct plan at the outset.

The other is returns. As long as interest rates stay low, the tax-sheltered profits from savings and GIC-based TFSAs will be minimal. That can add up to a lot of money over time. If you contribute $5500 a year to a GIC TFSA that earns an average of 2.5 percent annually, your plan will be worth $29,633 at the end of five years. But if you invest in mutual funds that generate an average annual gain of 6 percent, the plan will grow to $32,864—a difference of more than $3200.

Check the Costs

Many people don't think about the costs when opening a TFSA. They know they can take out the money tax-free, and that's all that concerns them. But expenses can add up, even on supposedly "free" plans, so make sure you understand all the fine print before you sign on the dotted line. Here are some costs to watch out for.

Transfer fees. These are assessed if you move part or all of your account to another financial institution. It may be as much as $150. In the case of self-directed plans, a few brokerage firms assess a fee for each security that is transferred.

Withdrawal fees. Most financial institutions allow free withdrawals from TFSAs, but some impose limits on the number you can make each year. There will be a charge if you exceed the maximum. In a very few cases, a company may charge a small fee, such as one to five dollars, for every withdrawal.

Closing fees. Although there is usually no charge for making a withdrawal, most financial institutions will hit you with a fee if you close the account entirely. The standard fee is $25 but it could be more.

Administration fees. These are generally applied only to self-directed plans. The fee is assessed annually and can range from as low as $25 to a percentage of the plan's assets, typically 1 percent.

Early redemption fees. If you terminate the plan within a short time after opening it (usually 30 days but sometimes as long as six months), you may be hit with this cost. It could come in the form of a direct charge or as loss of interest on an investment such as a redeemable GIC.

Contributions in kind. Some companies charge a fee for transferring securities directly into a TFSA. This is usually $25 to $50.

Sales commissions. These may be charged if you buy third-party mutual funds for a bank TFSA or any mutual funds in a self-directed plan. The amount is open to negotiation, and this should be done prior to setting up an account. My advice is to ask for front-end load units at zero commission. The salesperson won't like it because it means less money in her pocket but she will still receive the annual trailer fees on the funds you buy. You pay for these through the management fees and expenses that are assessed each year on your funds.

Brokerage commissions. If you have a self-directed plan, you may be charged commissions on all stock transactions. This can be avoided if you use a fee-based account.

ACTION SUMMARY

1. Understand the five different types of TFSAs and choose the plan that best fits your needs.
2. The wrong plan can cost you thousands in lost profits and could end up causing problems with the Canada Revenue Agency. Take the time needed to make the right choice.
3. Even "free" plans may have some fees and expenses attached to them that are buried in the small print. Ask questions about all the costs before proceeding.

15
TFSA Portfolios

It's not hard to convince people that TFSAs are a great idea. "Tax-free" is a term that catches everyone's attention. The main difficulty Canadians have is figuring out what to put into their plans. Here's an email I received from a Vancouver resident who wanted some specific recommendations for his TFSA:

> I know that you have several kinds of model portfolios in your newsletters and I know that everybody is different when it comes to investing. So please suggest a portfolio for a TFSA.

There is one major problem with this. It stems from the fact that TFSAs are so flexible. They can be used for any purpose: as an emergency fund, for short-term savings such as a home down payment, for longer-term savings, for retirement planning, for estate planning, and more. So there is no one-size-fits-all TFSA portfolio. Everything depends on your goals.

For example, if the plan is intended to be an emergency fund then the money should be invested in highly liquid, low-risk securities. These would include high-interest savings accounts, money market funds, mortgage funds, redeemable

GICs, and short-term bond funds. The return would be negligible in a low-interest-rate environment—perhaps 2 percent at best. But that's a secondary concern. The main objective is to build a cash reserve that's readily available in the event of a crisis such as a serious illness or job loss.

That's a much different approach than if you are using a TFSA to supplement retirement savings. In that case, the portfolio would be structured along the same lines as an RRSP with the twin goals of preserving capital and achieving a reasonable rate of growth over the long term.

One of the great advantages of a TFSA is that it's available to all adults—there is no age limit as there is with RRSPs. For anyone over 71, it's the simplest and most accessible tax shelter available. These people have yet another set of priorities. They tend to be more conservative in their outlook so they want to protect their capital, either with a view to drawing against it in future years or leaving it to their heirs. These portfolios will tend to favour bonds or bond funds with perhaps some blue-chip stocks added to the mix for income and modest growth.

The upshot is that not only is there no one TFSA portfolio that is suitable for everyone, but it is impossible to create one that would meet the needs of even a majority of people. That said, I think it is important to offer some kind of guidance about these accounts. As of January 1, 2013, the cumulative contribution entitlement of anyone who was 18 when the plans were launched in 2009 will have reached $25,500. That's $51,000 for a couple, so we're at the stage where the potential investment has become meaningful.

So I have put together several sample portfolios that you can use as guidelines to create a TFSA that meets your needs. These do not contain any recommendations for specific securities. I mention several stocks and funds, but they are meant to be examples only. The investment scene is constantly changing, so it's best to consult with a financial adviser before acting. A stock that looked great in 2012 may be a dog by 2014 due to unforeseen developments.

That's why these portfolios are generic in nature. They include the types of securities and the appropriate asset mix for each situation. You choose the investments that fit best. Make sure your plan is appropriate for the specific securities you want (e.g., self-directed).

An Emergency Fund TFSA

Here the priority is safety and liquidity. The rate of return is a secondary concern but should not be ignored. It is possible to squeeze out a little more profit from this type of plan than you might expect.

The key is not to put all the money into a high-interest savings account. By diversifying the plan you may add a small amount of risk but you will boost the return potential and generate more tax-sheltered income. Here are the components of the Emergency Fund TFSA. You'll need a multiple-option plan or a self-directed plan to implement it.

High-interest savings account. This should be the foundation stone of the portfolio. All the money will be protected by deposit insurance and you'll have full access to it if required. Weighting: 40 percent.

No-load mortgage mutual fund. Mortgage funds rarely lose money—in fact, some never have. The National Bank Mortgage Fund has been in existence since August 1991. Its worst twelve-month period was for the year to the end of January 1995 when it gained only 0.51 percent. The HSBC Mortgage Fund has a similar story. It was launched in December 1992, and its worst year was a profit of 0.89 percent in the twelve months to June 30, 2006.

The returns from a typical mortgage fund will be only slightly more than what you'll get from a high-interest savings account but, in this portfolio, every little bit helps. Be sure to get a no-load fund to avoid sales commissions. Weighting: 30 percent.

No-load universe bond fund. There's a little more risk here but not a lot if you choose carefully. The worst twelve months in the history of the Phillips, Hager & North Total Return Bond Fund, which was started in July 2000, was a decline of 0.76 percent in the period ending February 28, 2009 (D units).

On the plus side, returns from a fund like this will usually be well in excess of anything you might earn in a savings account, thus giving this portfolio a nice boost. Choose a universe bond fund—one that invests in all types of fixed-income securities—for maximum diversification. Weighting: 30 percent.

Here's what this portfolio would look like.

Emergency Fund TFSA Portfolio

Type of security	Weight %
High-interest savings account	40
No-load mortgage mutual fund	30
No-load universe bond mutual fund	30
Total	100

Summary. This portfolio offers all the elements needed for an emergency fund. The risk is very low, all the assets are highly liquid (you can cash in no-load fund units at any time without penalty), and the return will be higher than you'll earn by putting all the money into a savings account.

A Savings TFSA

This is a plan for those who are using a TFSA to save for a specific purchase such as a car or a house down payment and have a time horizon of two to five years. (If your time frame is shorter, use the Emergency Fund TFSA Portfolio.)

Here, preservation of capital will be important but we will also aim for a somewhat higher return. This is feasible because liquidity is not as essential as it is in an emergency fund when cash might be required at any time. The components of this portfolio follow.

No-load short-term bond mutual fund. These funds invest in fixed-income securities that mature within five years. They rarely lose money but they are not entirely risk-free. In a bad year, such a fund might drop a percent or two in value, but that's a risk that's acceptable in the context of the improved return potential compared to a high-interest savings account. This fund will be the cornerstone of this portfolio. Weighting: 40 percent.

No-load universe bond mutual fund. This one has somewhat more risk than the short-term bond fund but higher return potential. Weighting: 30 percent.

No-load dividend mutual fund. This is the potential growth engine of the portfolio. These funds invest mainly in blue-chip, dividend-paying common stocks, although some also hold lower-risk preferred shares. If stock markets dive, as they did in 2008–2009, this fund will be vulnerable to potentially significant losses (say, 20 to 30 percent). But that is rare. Under normal conditions, we should expect an average annual return in the 6-percent range from a fund of this type. Weighting: 30 percent.

This is what your portfolio should look like.

Savings TFSA Portfolio

Type of security	Weight %
No-load short-term bond mutual fund	40
No-load universe bond mutual fund	30
No-load dividend mutual fund	30
Total	100

Summary. This portfolio offers more growth potential but contains somewhat more risk as well. To minimize the risk, cash in the dividend fund when you are within six months of making your purchase, unless the stock market is in a rebound phase from an earlier correction.

An Education Savings TFSA

Although an RESP is the best way to save for a child's education, some people may want to use a TFSA to add to the amount being put aside or to avoid the risk of a heavy tax penalty if the student does not go on to post-secondary education.

In this case, some careful management of the money is required. During the early years, the portfolio should be growth-oriented with a relatively small fixed-income component. As the child approaches college age, the percentage of fixed-income assets should be increased to reduce the risk of loss in the event of a stock market crash. By the time the student has finished high school, almost all of the fund should be in fixed-income securities or cash.

In this case, therefore, we'll look at three different portfolios, one for each stage of the child's growth, starting with birth to age 10. These are the key components at this point. Note: Wherever possible, use no-load mutual funds or front-end load units purchased at zero commission.

High-interest savings account. It's a good idea to keep a small amount of cash in reserve to be able to take advantage of opportunities, such as a stock market correction that creates some good bargains. Weighting: 5 percent.

Canadian stock mutual fund/ETF. A fund with a strong track record that invests in top Canadian companies should be the foundation for this plan. Because of the relatively long time horizon, it doesn't matter if it is a mutual fund or an exchange-traded fund. What you're looking for are above-average returns with below-average risk. Some examples are Beutel Goodman Canadian Equity Fund, CI Signature Select Canadian Fund, Fidelity Canadian Large Cap Fund, iShares S&P/TSX 60 Index ETF, Mawer Canadian Equity Fund, and RBC North American Value Fund. Weighting: 30 percent.

U.S. stock mutual fund/ETF. The American stock market is much more broadly diversified than ours and is the strongest in the world. During the first decade of the 2000s, Canadians received very little profit from U.S. stocks because of the rapid rise of the loonie, but that is highly unlikely to happen again. In both 2011 and 2012, the main U.S. indexes outperformed the S&P/TSX Composite Index by a wide margin. So a U.S. equity fund should boost this portfolio's returns. Examples of funds with good long-term track records include Altamira U.S. Currency Neutral Index Fund, Dynamic American Value Fund, iShares S&P 500 Index ETF, RBC U.S. Dividend Fund, and TD U.S. Index Currency Neutral Fund. Weighting: 30 percent.

International stock mutual fund/ETF. We will add an international fund to this portfolio to provide exposure to the growing overseas markets. International funds did not do well during the 2010–2012 period because of the slow recovery from the credit crisis and ongoing problems in Europe. But they should fare better going forward. Some decent performers are Counsel International Growth Fund, Manulife World Investment Class, and Mawer International Equity Fund. Weighting: 10 percent.

Canadian small/mid-cap mutual fund/ETF. Small- to mid-cap stocks tend to have better returns than blue-chip equities, but they also come with more risk. Therefore, we are keeping the weighting to a minimum, although we do want some exposure to this sector. Choices to consider include Beutel Goodman Small Cap Fund, Bissett Canadian High Dividend Fund, Dynamic Small Business Fund, Ethical Special Equity Fund, and Fidelity Canadian Opportunities Fund. Weighting: 5 percent.

Universe bond mutual fund/ETF. All portfolios should have some fixed-income exposure, so use a universe bond fund or ETF to round out this one. Weighting: 20 percent.

Here's what the portfolio will look like:

Education Savings TFSA Portfolio (Age 0–10)

Type of security	Weight %
High-interest savings account	5
Canadian stock mutual fund/ETF	30
U.S. stock mutual fund/ETF	30
International stock mutual fund/ETF	10
Canadian small/mid-cap mutual fund/ETF	5
Universe bond mutual fund/ETF	20
Total	100

As the child gets older, the portfolio should become more conservative to protect against big losses. This can be done gradually. Here are guidelines you can use:

Education Savings TFSA Portfolio (Age 11–14)

Type of security	Weight %
High-interest savings account	10
Canadian stock mutual fund/ETF	25
U.S. stock mutual fund/ETF	25
International stock mutual fund/ETF	5
Universe bond mutual fund/ETF	35
Total	100

As the teen nears college age, adjust the portfolio to emphasize safety and liquidity so that the money will be available when the time comes to move on to post-secondary schooling. The stock funds should be sold off as market conditions permit and the money redirected to fixed-income funds and high-interest savings. Here's what stage three of this portfolio might look like:

Education Savings TFSA Portfolio (Age 15–18)

Type of security	Weight %
High-interest savings account	15
Short-term bond fund/ETF	35
Universe bond mutual fund/ETF	25
Canadian stock mutual fund/ETF	15
U.S. stock mutual fund/ETF	10
Total	100

At this point, the student is ready for college, so it's time to remove almost all the risk and put most of the assets into cash so that the funds are available as needed.

Education Savings TFSA Portfolio (Age 19+)

Type of security	Weight %
High-interest savings account	50
Short-term bond fund/ETF	50
Total	100

Summary. This type of portfolio requires more active management than the others we have looked at thus far, but it offers a very effective way of building a college fund. The same parameters could be used in a self-directed RESP.

A Retirement Savings TFSA

If you plan to use a TFSA for retirement savings, the overriding principle at all times is to treat it like a pension plan. That means keeping risk to a minimum, using a conservative approach to your investment selections, and maintaining a significant weighting in fixed-income securities.

As with the Education Savings Portfolio, the asset mix should vary over time with the risk component gradually being reduced as retirement age nears. In this case, the time horizon is much longer, however.

The basic components of a Retirement Savings TFSA are the same as those used in the Education Saving Portfolio. But in this case, you can consider using individual stocks instead of equity mutual funds or ETFs as the amount of money in the plan increases. If you decide to go the stock market route, stick with Canadian and American dividend-paying blue-chip securities. Some examples from the Toronto Stock Exchange include BCE Inc., CN Rail, Enbridge, TransCanada Corporation, and the major banks. In the U.S., stocks like AT&T, Walmart, McDonald's, Johnson & Johnson, Microsoft, General Electric, Walt Disney Company, and Procter & Gamble are all suitable for a retirement plan.

Here's a sample portfolio for someone aged 20 to 25. It's on the conservative side, which I think is important for someone just starting out. "Funds" may include mutual funds or ETFs. See Chapter 13 for an explanation of variable-income funds.

Retirement Savings TFSA Portfolio (Age 20–25)

Type of security	Weight %
High-interest savings account	5
Canadian blue-chip stocks/funds	25
U.S. blue-chip stocks/funds	25
International funds	5
Variable-income funds	10
Fixed-income funds	30
Total	100

Assuming you start early, by the time you reach 25, you should have a better idea of what you're doing and how to choose appropriate investments. At this stage, you can start being a little more aggressive in your approach by adding some small/mid-cap holdings with the aim of improving returns.

Retirement Savings TFSA Portfolio (Age 26–49)

Type of security	Weight %
High-interest savings account	5
Canadian blue-chip stocks/funds	25
U.S. blue-chip stocks/funds	25
International funds	10
Small/mid-cap stocks/funds	5
Variable-income funds	10
Fixed-income funds	20
Total	100

Once you pass 50, start being a little more conservative, but the emphasis should continue to be on growth. Here's an example. I've dropped the small/mid-cap and international categories and added the weight to the fixed-income assets and cash.

Retirement Savings TFSA Portfolio (Age 50–59)

Type of security	Weight %
High-interest savings account	10
Canadian blue-chip stocks/funds	25
U.S. blue-chip stocks/funds	25
Variable-income funds	10
Fixed-income funds	30
Total	100

By the time you reach 60, retirement is looming. It's time to start preparing by ratcheting down risk, raising the fixed-income allocation (e.g., bonds, bond funds, GICs), and adding some cash, either in the form of money market funds or a high-interest savings account. However, don't eliminate the growth component entirely as it will provide some inflation protection.

Retirement Savings TFSA Portfolio (Age 60–65)

Type of security	Weight %
High-interest savings account	10
Canadian blue-chip stocks/funds	20
U.S. blue-chip stocks/funds	15
Variable-income funds	15
Fixed-income funds	40
Total	100

If you have not retired at age 65 and don't need the cash in the plan immediately, you can continue to build this TFSA. But the portfolio should become increasingly conservative as retirement approaches. This is what it might look like in the final year before you plan to retire:

Retirement Savings TFSA Portfolio (Age 66+)

Type of security	Weight %
High-interest savings account	15
Canadian blue-chip stocks/funds	10
U.S. blue-chip stocks/funds	10
Variable-income funds	15
Fixed-income funds	50
Total	100

Summary. Although I have shown five portfolios, there are really two principal stages to a successful retirement plan. The first is the growth stage during which you take some additional risk in order to hopefully generate above-average gains. This lasts until about age fifty. Stage two is consolidation and preservation. If you have done a good job and started early enough, your plan will be worth tens or even hundreds of thousands of dollars by the time you enter your fifties. Now you want to ease back the throttle a little and ensure that you don't suffer a major setback. By the time you're ready to pack it in, much of the risk is removed, and you have a secure nest egg.

A Post-Retirement TFSA

As mentioned earlier in the book, there is no age limit for holding a Tax-Free Savings Account. That makes them especially valuable to older Canadians, who must terminate their RRSPs by December 31 of the year in which they turn 71. At that point a TFSA becomes the only low-cost, easily accessible tax shelter available to them.

At this stage in life, capital preservation and liquidity become the most important priorities for most people. Any growth is a bonus. Therefore, this portfolio should focus on low-risk securities, which should include a significant amount of cash.

A useful strategy to consider at this point is laddered bonds or GICs. This involves investing a specific dollar amount in securities that mature annually over a number of years, usually five. This way, there is always some cash becoming available.

For example, suppose you have $25,000 that you want to invest in GICs. Put $5000 of that into a one-year certificate, another $5000 into a two-year certificate, and so on out to five years. There are several advantages to this:

1. The blended interest rate you receive will be more than if you put everything into a one-year GIC and kept rolling it over.
2. If interest rates move higher, you will have $5000 maturing each year to reinvest at a higher rate.
3. If you need to withdraw money, you'll be able to access $5000 plus interest each year.

Unless you want to eliminate virtually all risk, keep a small amount of the portfolio in growth securities to provide an inflation hedge.

Here is what a conservative Post-Retirement TFSA Portfolio might look like:

Post Retirement TFSA Portfolio

Type of security	Weight %
High-interest savings account	15
Fixed-income funds/GICs	65
Canadian stocks/funds	10
U.S. stocks/funds	10
Total	100

Summary. Don't expect high returns from this portfolio. When interest rates are low, an annual gain of 3 percent to 5 percent is the best you are likely to achieve. But that's better than leaving the money in a savings account, and it's all tax-free.

A Tax-Savings Maximizer TFSA

Finally, let's consider a model TFSA portfolio for aggressive investors—those who want to use the plan to maximize the tax-free gains and who are willing to accept the risks associated with that. The main focus will be on capital gains, which offer the greatest potential for tax-free profits.

This approach runs counter to traditional advice that suggests keeping securities that generate dividends and capital gains in non-registered accounts to benefit from the tax breaks accorded those types of investment income. Use tax shelters for interest-bearing securities that are taxed at marginal rates, the rationale suggests.

However, when interest rates are low, the amount of profit that would be tax-sheltered by using the traditional approach is negligible. Even if you were able to generate a 4 percent return, that would only amount to $400 on a $10,000 investment. By contrast, if you could earn a 20 percent capital gain on that money, it would be worth $2000. In a non-registered account, $1000 of that would be taxable at your marginal rate. A TFSA allows you to keep it all.

If this is the approach you are looking for in your TFSA, your focus will have to be on individual stocks, aggressively managed mutual funds, and ETFs that specialize in high-growth sectors. You will need a self-directed plan with a brokerage firm to have access to the full range of options.

This is what you might call a "handle with care" portfolio. Do not attempt it unless you are knowledgeable about investing, willing to devote some time to managing it, and can live with the risk involved. All of the securities are equity-based, which means that if we have another stock market crash as in 2008–2009 this portfolio will get clobbered. On the other hand, if stocks rise, there is a good likelihood of significant capital gains.

Here are the main components:

High-growth stocks. You're looking for equities with superior growth potential—remember the primary goal is to generate capital gains. Shopping for bargains when markets are down after a sharp correction is one of the best ways to achieve this. Often, the best growth stocks are ones you have never heard of—fast-growing, small- and mid-cap companies that are well-managed and have earnings momentum. Read the business press and/or subscribe to a high-quality investment newsletter for ideas. You're looking for companies that have the potential to be the next Google or Apple.

Some Canadian stocks that we have identified as having above-average growth potential in my *Internet Wealth Builder* newsletter are auto parts manufacturer Linamar; robotics and space engineering company MacDonald Dettwiller; up-and-coming airline WestJet; and Vancouver-based Westport

Innovations, which is a leader in developing technology to convert diesel-fuelled vehicles to natural gas.

In the United States, we feel eBay, fast-food giant Yum! Brands, high-tech company Broadcom, and railway firm Norfolk Southern all have good growth prospects.

Aggressive mutual funds. There are several actively-managed funds that specialize in high-growth stocks in such volatile sectors as mining and energy. When they are going well, they can produce huge gains. The converse is true when the markets turn against them. An example is the Front Street Growth Fund. It lost 57 percent over the year ending February 28, 2009, as world stock markets plunged and commodity prices tanked. Then it turned around and gained an astounding 131 percent in the next 12 months as markets rallied. That's the kind of roller-coaster ride you can expect in a fund of this type.

If you prefer something a little less adventurous, look for a more diversified fund that holds some blue-chip stocks in combination with smaller companies.

Dynamic Power Canadian Growth Fund is one example.

Sector ETFs. Exchange-traded funds originally were designed to track major stock indexes such as the Dow and the S&P/TSX Composite. But the rapid growth of the industry has resulted in the creation of a wide range of specialized funds, some of which offer very good growth potential—with the attendant risk, of course. Here are three examples:

iShares S&P/TSX SmallCap Index Fund (TSX: XCS).
This ETF tracks the index of the same name. The stocks are
selected by Standard & Poor's using its industrial classifications
and guidelines for evaluating issuer capitalization, liquidity,
and fundamentals. There were 253 holdings in the portfolio
at the time of writing, and no stock accounted for more than
1.97 percent of total assets. The MER is 0.55 percent. Its
worst twelve-month period ended February 28, 2009, with
a loss of 48 percent. In the subsequent year, it rebounded by
75 percent.

**BMO NASDAQ 100 Equity Hedged to CAD Index ETF
(TSX: ZQQ).** Technology companies came back into favour
following the 2008–2009 crash. This ETF provides exposure
to the top 100 stocks on the tech-heavy NASDAQ exchange,
hedged back to Canadian dollars. The management fee is
0.35 percent. This fund was launched in January 2010, after
the markets had recovered from the 2008–2009 collapse, so
there is not much history to work with at this stage.

iShares BRIC Index Fund (TSX: CBQ). No aggressive
stock portfolio would be complete without some exposure to
the fast-developing BRIC nations (Brazil, Russia, India, and
China). This ETF emulates the BNY Mellon BRIC Select ADR
Index, which tracks the performance of companies from these
countries that trade in New York as American Depository
Receipts (ADRs) or Global Depository Receipts (GDRs). Like
all emerging-markets funds, this one had a rough time in
2008, losing 58 percent. It rebounded well in 2009 with a

gain of 75 percent, which gives some idea of the volatility you have to expect. The MER is on the high side at 0.67 percent.

You can mix and match these in a portfolio in any way you like but here is what I would suggest:

Tax-Savings Maximizer TFSA Portfolio

Type of security	Weight %
Canadian growth stocks	30
U.S. growth stocks	30
Canadian growth ETFs	15
U.S. growth ETFs	15
Aggressive mutual funds	10
Total	100

Summary. I caution again that this portfolio is suitable only for experienced investors who can deal with high volatility. It's a high-risk/high-return approach to TFSA management. The securities need to be traded actively to achieve the best results, so if you are a buy-and-hold type, choose a different strategy.

ACTION SUMMARY

1. Decide what your main savings objective is before opening a TFSA.
2. Choose a plan that is appropriate to your goals.

3. Decide on an appropriate asset allocation, using the model portfolios in this chapter as guidelines.
4. Select specific securities that meet the criteria you have established.
5. Monitor the portfolio at least quarterly and replace underperforming securities.
6. Stay on plan. Don't get sidetracked.

16
Your TFSA Questions

At first glance, the concept of Tax-Free Savings Accounts appears to be dead simple. You put money in and then later you take it out, just like with a bank savings account. What could be easier?

But things are not always as they seem, and TFSAs are a lot more complicated than that. I have been surprised by the hundreds of questions that have flooded my email inbox since the launch of the TFSA program on January 1, 2009. Initially, I thought it was because people were still trying to come to grips with the new plans. But that was several years ago and the questions keep coming. It's pretty clear at this point that there are a lot of nuances and subtleties to TFSAs that many Canadians have not been able to grasp.

This should not be a surprise. RRSPs have been around for more than half a century, but I still receive many questions about them each year. The reality is that all government programs come with a lot of regulatory baggage that people have to deal with. Moreover, bureaucrats and politicians have a habit of frequently tinkering with the rules, creating more confusion in the process.

So, if you have questions about Tax-Free Savings Accounts, you can take comfort in the knowledge that you are not alone. Thousands of other Canadians are in the same boat.

This chapter contains some of the questions I have received, divided into subject categories. If you're still puzzled by something, scan through the list of topics and see if you can find the answer to your own question. If not, send it to me at Gordon.Pape@BuildingWealth.ca and type "TFSA book question" in the subject line. I can't provide personal answers, but replies to selected questions will be posted on www.BuildingWealth.ca and in my newsletters.

Note: Some of the questions refer to a $5000 annual contribution, which was the maximum allowed from 2009 to 2012. It was expected that the limit would rise to $5500 on January 1, 2013.

Basic Rules

HOW MANY TFSAs?

Q I would like to know if I can have more than one TFSA as long as the total contribution to all of them does not exceed the annual maximum.

A You can open as many TFSAs as you want, just as you can with RRSPs. However, be sure you really need more than one, because each account means more paperwork and makes keeping track of the investments more complicated. Also, ask about fees before opening a plan. Some financial institutions have no TFSA administration fees for certain types of plans. A no-fee plan will add to your return.

DELAYING TFSAs

Q I have two sons in university. I have their upcoming tuition covered with RESPs and in-trust accounts. At this time, they pay no tax because of their tuition deductions, so any money they receive interest on is tax-free. Is it okay to wait and allow them to add to their TFSAs once they are employed (I hope); that is, can they deposit the $5000 per year "retroactively" when they have the money themselves in future years, or do they lose the ability to deposit the $5000 if they do not do it in the year it is eligible?

A TFSAs have the same carry-forward privileges as RRSPs. It is not a "use it or lose it" situation; if contribution room is not used in a given year, it is added to the next year's limit. So your sons can wait until they have their own cash to open accounts. However, they will lose out on the years of tax-free compounding until then.

TFSAs AS COLLATERAL

Q Can I use my TFSA as collateral?

A Yes. This is one of the major differences between Tax-Free Savings Accounts and RRSPs. The assets within a TFSA may be pledged as collateral against a loan. However, by doing so, you may find that you will be prohibited from making withdrawals as long as the loan is outstanding.

TFSA CARRY-FORWARDS

Q My mom went to a seminar and was told that the contribution room only begins to accumulate after you open a TFSA. That is, if you don't open an account until 2014, you will only be allowed to deposit $5500 because you didn't earn the contribution room in previous years. I am wondering whether she is correct (although I will be opening a TFSA in the near future, just to be on the safe side).

A The information she received is incorrect. You don't have to open an account to accumulate contribution room. As long as you are age 18 or older, your TFSA contribution room will be credited to you. If you don't use it, the amount will be added to the next year's contribution limit.

If you file an income tax return, the Canada Revenue Agency will keep track of your available contribution room and include the information in your personal account, which can be accessed through the My Account link on their website.

WHEN DO CARRY-FORWARDS START?

Q I am not sure if the carry-forward of unused contribution room starts when you open your first account or did it start with the introduction of the Tax-Free Savings Account program itself? For example, if I open my first TFSA account in 2013, will I have a $25,000 contribution limit at that time?

A Canadians begin accumulating TFSA contribution room at age 18, with 2009 being year one of the program. You don't have to open an account or even file a tax return. Assuming you are age 18 or older now and don't open a

TFSA until 2013, as you suggest, at that point you will have accumulated four years of carry-forward room (2009–2012), worth $20,000. Add another $5500 for 2013 and you'll be able to contribute $25,500 that year.

SPOUSAL TFSAs

Q Can I set up a spousal TFSA? Do I need to? Since the income-attribution rules don't apply, why wouldn't the spouse with money simply give funds to the other to set up a plan in his or her own name?

A There is no such thing as a spousal TFSA, unlike the situation with RRSPs. Neither are there joint plans. Each person's TFSA is his or her own. So you are correct—one spouse can simply give money to the other to open his or her own plan.

It has been suggested that this creates a way to shift significant assets from one spouse to another over time. For example, a husband might give his wife $5500 to open a plan in 2013. In December, she withdraws the $5500, which is then added to the next year's contribution limit, making it $11,000. He then gives her $11,000 to contribute and the process is repeated annually. On the surface, this would enable her to build a large non-registered investment account as well as a TFSA.

However, the government anticipated this loophole by adding a line that says the attribution rules "will not apply to income earned in a TFSA that is derived from such contributions."[1] Note the phrase "in a TFSA," which suggests that if the money is withdrawn by the spouse and then reinvested, the attribution rules will kick in. We may see a court challenge on this one.

RESIDENCY ISSUES

Q There is a question I have with regard to eligibility. Our son is a full-time medical student, age 23, a Canadian citizen and a Canadian resident, has a Social Insurance Number, and has filed income-tax returns since he was 18 years old. We wish to open TFSAs for our entire family of four but were recently told by our financial adviser that our son is not eligible, since he is "not a permanent resident" of Canada as he is currently studying in the United States. Please advise! Is he ineligible just because he is temporarily studying in the United States?

A Residency status can be somewhat tricky. However, if your son files Canadian tax returns, does not own property in the United States, and returns to Canada during summer breaks, there is a strong case to be made that he is in fact a Canadian resident. A fact sheet on TFSAs from the Canada Revenue Agency states as follows:

> *Even if you no longer live in Canada, you may have residential ties in Canada that are sufficient for you to be considered a factual or deemed resident of Canada. In these cases, the regular rules for opening a TFSA still apply. Residential ties include a home in Canada; a spouse or common-law partner or dependants in Canada; personal property in Canada, such as a car or furniture; or social ties in Canada. Other ties that may be relevant include:*

a Canadian driver's licence; Canadian bank accounts or credit cards; and hospitalization and medical insurance coverage from a province or territory of Canada.[2]

The CRA says that additional information can be found in Interpretation Bulletin IT-221R, Determination of an Individual's Residence Status.[3]

TFSA PROFITS

Q Suppose I invest $5000 in a Tax-Free Savings Account through a bank using their online brokerage service and I make $2000 in three months on stocks. Can I reinvest the $7000 or can I just reinvest the original $5000?

A As long as you do not withdraw the money from the TFSA, you can reinvest all profits earned within the plan at any time. There are no restrictions.

TREATMENT OF WITHDRAWALS

Q I wanted to use my TFSA to cover monthly bills, followed by topping up when the pension cheque arrives. The man at the bank said that the first time I topped up, the CRA would consider that I had overcontributed and assess a penalty. Presumably, by his reckoning, if a person did this each month, one could wind up with a very sizeable overcontribution at year-end.

Is this guy right? It sounds pretty implausible in these days when the net deposit amount for a given year can be easily calculated and transmitted to CRA should it exceed the allowable maximum.

A Yes, he is correct. Any withdrawals cannot be recontributed to the plan until the following year.

ADVANCE CONTRIBUTIONS

Q I have already contributed the maximum for this year and invested in stocks. However, I would like to make another contribution at this time for the next year. Can I contribute in advance?

A No. If you contribute any more money to your plan between now and January 1 of next year, it will be considered an overcontribution. Any profits made on income earned from overcontributions will be taxed at a rate of 100 percent as a result of changes to the Income Tax Act announced in October 2009.

OVERCONTRIBUTIONS

Q My friend withdrew $5000 from his TFSA, and in the same year he deposited $5000 back into his TFSA. He was told by the bank he would have to pay a fine to the Canada Revenue Agency. My question is what percentage is the fine for $5000? I know there is no penalty if you deposit the money you withdrew the following year.

A If the overcontribution was an honest mistake, the fine is 1 percent per month of the total amount in excess of the contribution limit at the start of the year. So if your friend had a $5000 contribution limit when the year began, then the fine is one percent of $5000 per month or $50. That will continue until the excess is withdrawn from the plan or until he gets enough new contribution room to cover it (at the start of the following year).

The situation can become more complicated when a person makes multiple contributions and withdrawals in the same year. In its Guide to Tax-Free Savings Accounts for Individuals, the CRA cites the example of a fictional taxpayer named Judy who has a $5000 contribution limit at the start of the year. Over a 12-month period, here is what she does:

January 25	contributes $4000
March 16	contributes $1000
June 15	withdraws $2000
August 23	contributes $2000
September 8	withdraws $1000

This series of actions results in a TFSA nightmare for Judy. The January and March contributions covered her full allowance for the year. Her June withdrawal will not get added back to her contribution room until the following year, so her August contribution of $2000 created an excess TFSA amount for that month. Her September withdrawal of $1000 would be considered a qualifying withdrawal in computing her penalty interest for the following month, October. The excess of $1000 remains until the end of the year and she will have to pay a 1 percent tax on it for the months of August to December.

Her total penalty tax works out to 1 percent per month on $2000 for August and September, or $40, plus 1 percent per month on $1000 for October to December, or $30. Total: $70.

This is why I don't recommend making multiple deposits and withdrawals from a TFSA each year.

If you find yourself in this situation, you have to file Form RC243, Tax-Free Savings Account (TFSA) Return and Form RC243-SCH-A, Schedule A – Excess TFSA Amounts.

One more point: If the overcontribution is considered to be deliberate, the CRA will also level a tax of 100 percent on any profit earned from that money.

OVERCONTRIBUTION PENALTIES

Q The Canada Revenue Agency charges a 1 percent penalty per month or 12 percent a year on overcontributions to the account. But if your yield is higher than 12 percent, I wonder whether the difference is still tax-free? For example, does a contribution invested to yield 20 percent per year less 12 percent overcontribution penalty equal an 8-percent tax-free yield?

A That math worked until late October 2009. At that point, Finance Minister Jim Flaherty announced amendments to the Income Tax Act that imposed a 100-percent tax on any profits earned as a result of overcontributions. So forget the whole idea!

MOVING TFSA ASSETS

Q I have a TFSA account with TD Bank and my investment account with TD Waterhouse. Can I move TFSA funds to my general non-registered investment account or do these funds have to remain segregated? If the latter, does this mean

I need another TFSA account with TD Waterhouse, or does the TFSA account with TD Bank need to be transferred?

My example is for TD, but I imagine the question applies to all the big banks with separate investment arms.

A The only way you could move TFSA money into your non-registered investment account is to withdraw it, which I assume is not what you want to do, as you would lose the tax-sheltering.

You could open a new TFSA with TD Waterhouse and transfer some or all of the assets from the bank into it, as there is no limit on the number of plans you can have. However, ask if a transfer fee will apply.

TFSAs AND CLAWBACKS

Q My question relates to TFSA withdrawals. When you withdraw money from your TFSA at 65 and beyond, does the government factor in the amount when calculating any clawbacks on pension income?

A No. TFSA withdrawals are not considered as income (unlike RRSP or RRIF withdrawals). This means they do not affect the Old Age Security clawback nor do they penalize people who qualify for the Guaranteed Income Supplement. This is one reason why these plans are especially suitable for older Canadians.

Death and TFSAs

SUCCESSOR ACCOUNT HOLDERS

Q I had an incredibly confusing time designating my husband and me as "successor account holders" for each other's newly opened Tax-Free Savings Accounts. Our broker refused to allow the "successor" designation to be placed on our accounts. We would greatly appreciate a reply from you clarifying exactly what it is that we can do.

A Succession laws are provincial responsibilities, so although the federal rules clearly allow for a "successor account holder," the provinces each had to pass legislation to actually make it work. Some moved more quickly than others—Ontario, for example, did not implement the needed changes until mid-2009.

All the provinces and territories except Quebec are now onside, but action is required in the case of accounts that were opened before the enabling provincial legislation was passed. In such cases, go back to the plan administrator and complete the necessary documentation.

JOINT TFSAs

Q My wife and I share everything jointly: our real estate, our investments, our bank accounts. Is it possible to open a joint TFSA account? And if not, in the event of the demise of either of us, would the beneficiary (the other spouse) be liable for taxation on the accrued amount?

A Joint TFSAs are not permitted (nor are joint RRSPs for that matter). Each account must be in an individual name. If one spouse dies, the other will acquire the assets tax-free. The most effective way to do this is for each spouse to name the other as "successor account holder."

HUSBAND DIED, BANK CONFUSED

Q My husband passed away on May 17, 2009. He had a TFSA with our bank. The chequing and savings accounts are now in my name. It seems that my bank does not know what to do with his $5000. Any ideas?

A My condolences on your loss. It sounds like he did not designate you as a successor holder or beneficiary before he died. Perhaps this was because your province of residence had not approved enabling legislation.

The assets in the plan should pass to you tax-free nonetheless, but they might have to be processed as part of his estate, depending on the laws in your province. You should speak to a lawyer who specializes in this field.

TFSA BENEFICIARIES

Q How does survivorship affect the TFSA if you include children and spouse as beneficiaries in the TFSA account or through a will? Are there any probate fees to be paid?

A As I said in reply to the previous question, succession laws are governed by the provinces, so the situation will depend on where you live. However, in all provinces except Quebec, you can now designate a spouse/partner as a successor holder, which you should do. This ensures the assets in a TFSA will pass to the spouse/partner without having to wait for the estate to be settled and with no probate fees. Do not designate your spouse and children as joint beneficiaries, as that could create some legal problems.

General Strategies

SWITCHING TFSAs

Q I would now like to switch from a high-interest savings account to having some U.S. dividend-paying stocks in the account. Is it as simple as closing the existing account and setting up a self-directed TFSA, or are there special rules/ penalties surrounding this sort of change?

A You need to be careful if you have already made your maximum TFSA contribution for this year. If you withdraw the money from the account, you will not be able to recontribute it until January 1 of next year. At that time, the withdrawal will be added to next year's contribution allowance.

However, you can transfer the money directly into a new plan at the same financial institution if it offers a brokerage service, or another one without running into this problem. There may be a fee for closing the existing account.

But are you sure you really want to do this? Gena Katz, executive director, Tax Practice, at the accounting firm of Ernst & Young, says that the United States does not recognize TFSAs as registered plans when it comes to withholding tax on dividends. That means that 15 percent of all U.S. stock dividends paid into a TFSA will be withheld at source. (RRSPs and RRIFs are exempt from this withholding under the Canada-U.S. Tax Treaty.)

Maybe you should think this through again.

BALANCING ACT

Q I work on contract. Currently, my income stream is fine until the contract expires in September. I can always try to get contract work again, although it is not guaranteed. I wonder about my priorities in managing my finances. Should I build my cash reserve, make an RRSP contribution, or make a lump-sum payment against my mortgage? I have cash for four months of living expenses right now.

A Given the uncertainty of your situation, I suggest adding to your cash reserve. You may want to consider opening a Tax-Free Savings Account and keeping your emergency money there so as to eliminate taxes on the interest. Just make sure you don't lock in to a GIC in case you need to withdraw money.

If your employment situation becomes more stable, you can then withdraw some of that TFSA cash and make an RRSP contribution. Use the refund it will produce to make a mortgage payment. Yes, it's a balancing act, but it works.

NEEDS TFSA MONEY FOR DAUGHTER

Q My husband and I opened two individual TFSAs, depositing $5000 each. Since then we have found out that our daughter has been accepted in a post-graduate program. We did promise her a while back that we would help her out with tuition. Now the question is this: Can we withdraw some of the funds at the beginning of each semester and apply the proceeds against her tuition and reinvest the same amount prior to the year-end? For instance, this year we would withdraw money from the TFSAs in September, and by December we will redeposit the same amount in the same TFSAs, repeating this procedure semester after semester.

A Sorry, your plan won't work. You are allowed to replace the money you withdraw from a TFSA but not until the next calendar year. If you redeposit the cash in December, it will be considered an overcontribution, and you'll be faced with a tax of 100 percent on any profits earned from that extra money.

USE TFSA TO PAY MORTGAGE?

Q I am wondering if it would be strategic to invest $5500 in a TFSA now, withdraw the total funds in December, and put the proceeds against my mortgage. Next January, I would invest $11,000 in my TFSA and in December withdraw the total amount to pay against my mortgage, repeating this strategy year after year.

A This approach makes sense only if the rate of return you achieve within the Tax-Free Savings Account is higher than the interest rate on your mortgage. For example, if your mortgage rate is 4 percent but you can earn only 3 percent within your TFSA, you would be better off applying the $5500 against the mortgage principal immediately rather than waiting.

Finding the Money

TFSA SAVINGS

Q We are very intrigued by Tax-Free Savings Accounts—savings with no strings attached. But to contribute $5000 each per year (so a total of $10,000) would require a contribution of approximately $833/month. I'm not sure how we would find the financial resources to do that. How would you recommend going about this?

A Most Canadians receive an income tax refund each year. If you are among them, use that money to start a TFSA for each of you. That will reduce the additional monthly contribution you need, perhaps significantly.

Investment Options

RETURNS ON TFSAs

Q We've done some research but couldn't find any institution offering a competitive rate of return on a TFSA. Most are offering a maximum of 3 percent, so how would we get close to a 6-percent average rate of return?

A You're operating under the assumption that the money in a TFSA must be invested in some type of deposit account. That is not the case. TFSAs are like RRSPs in that there are several different types of plans. If you want to aim for a higher rate of return, choose a plan that allows you to invest in mutual funds or a self-directed plan that enables you to buy almost any type of security.

LOOKING FOR CERTAINTY

Q If we aim for a 6-percent return, can we be certain that the 6-percent interest rate would stick over the course of 20 to 25 years?

A You can't be certain of a 6-percent return, certainly not in the form of interest payments. These days, you're lucky to earn 3 percent on a five-year GIC. But you can expect to average at least 6 percent over the long haul by investing in a good-quality balanced fund or buying some high-grade corporate bonds and blue-chip dividend-paying stocks.

TFSAs AND GICs

Q I had a GIC that became redeemable. I saw my investment adviser at the bank and asked that this GIC be transferred into a TFSA. She advised me not to do this but rather to reinvest into the same GIC so that I would not have to pay the tax on accrued interest. I would appreciate your comments.

A I do not see what the problem is. The interest you earned is taxable—that's clear. You can now take the cash from the redeemed GIC, deposit it into your TFSA (to your contribution limit), and invest in a new GIC inside the plan if that is your wish. The interest earned on the new GIC will be tax-sheltered within the TFSA.

SAVING FOR RETIREMENT

Q Do you have any specific advice/guidelines on what type of vehicles/recommended fund groups to hold in my

Tax-Free Savings Account? I am a 42-year-old, married, self-employed mother of two. I plan to use all funds in my TFSA as part of my retirement plan. Thank you for any guidance.

A My first comment is that you should probably make the maximum contribution to your RRSP before using a TFSA for retirement savings. You'll get a tax deduction for the RRSP, which a TFSA will not give you.

If you have done that, I suggest taking a conservative approach with your TFSA investments since this money is, in effect, part of your personal pension plan. Since the annual contribution limit is only $5500, it can be expensive and inefficient to try to create a diversified portfolio immediately. Therefore, I suggest you start with a low-risk balanced fund. After a couple of years, when the assets in the TFSA have grown, you can blend in a range of other securities if you wish.

MAWER FUND

Q What is your opinion of the Mawer Balanced Fund as an initial TFSA holding for a conservative growth investor? The component equity funds are all highly regarded, the component bond fund appears to be middle of the pack, and the MER is low.

A This is a fund of funds, meaning that it invests primarily in six other Mawer funds with the Mawer Canadian Bond Fund as the largest single holding. The Calgary-based Mawer organization is a boutique house that I have recommended for several years.

This particular fund is slotted into the Global Neutral Balanced category where it has been an above-average performer for all time frames from one to twenty years. I think it would be a fine TFSA choice for a low-risk investor.

WHERE TO INVEST?

Q I have money in a U.S. index fund. The amount I have exceeds $5500. I was thinking of putting $5500 in a Tax-Free Savings Account. My question: If I do open this type of account, do I have to contribute each month or could I make a one-time deposit of $5500 and just let it grow through interest? If I do this, what is the interest per month? One other question: Will I earn more by moving my money from a U.S. index fund to a TFSA, or should I leave my money in the U.S. index fund? I am not really sure which is the better investment.

A There is clearly still a lot of confusion about what TFSAs really are. That's not surprising—the same thing happens with RRSPs and they have been around for more than 50 years.

To be clear, TFSAs, RRSPs, and so on are not investments. They are simply tax-sheltered "boxes" into which you place investments. When you open a TFSA or an RRSP, it is empty. You then fill it with whatever you want, as long as the investment is allowed by the Canada Revenue Agency.

So this is not a choice between a U.S. index fund and a TFSA. You can move $5500 worth of fund units into a TFSA, provided you set up the right kind of plan. In this case, it appears a self-directed TFSA with a broker would be the most appropriate.

You do not have to make monthly contributions. You can deposit $5500 cash or make a "contribution in kind" of $5500 worth of fund units. But a word of caution: If your fund has lost money, don't do a direct transfer, since you will not be able to claim a capital loss. Sell $5500 worth and deposit the cash. Then you can claim a loss when you file your next return.

You also asked about the interest rate for a TFSA. That depends on what type of interest-bearing investment you choose, if you decide to switch from the U.S. index fund. If you don't want to stay in the fund, check around for options.

TFSA RATES

Q What is a usual interest rate banks offer for a TFSA?

A There is no "usual" rate. It depends on the type of plan and the financial institution you are dealing with. If you have a savings account type of TFSA, the current interest rate will be minimal. It should rise when interest rates generally move higher but that may not be for some time. If you invest in a GIC, the rate will depend on the term and the type of GIC (redeemable or non-redeemable). A market-linked GIC will carry no fixed interest rate. Also, smaller institutions usually offer better rates. Shop around.

Remember, a TFSA does not have to come with any interest rate. It depends on the plan and how you invest. If you choose a mutual fund plan or a self-directed plan, no interest rate will apply.

YOUNG PERSON WANTS TO GET STARTED

Q I am turning 22 soon and would like to start investing for retirement, buying a house, and paying off student loans. I want to invest $2000 to start and would like to withdraw the money in 10 years at the earliest.

I've talked with financial planners/investment specialists at Coast Capital Savings, BMO, TD, Scotiabank, and Royal Bank. However, I have found that they all offer similar mutual funds that charge about the same MERs.

I am an aggressive investor (based on these financial institutions' questionnaires) and would like to maximize capital gains for the long term. Are there any specific mutual funds you recommend to be put in a Tax-Free Savings Account? Since I have only $2000 to invest right now, should I buy one or two mutual funds?

A Congratulations for understanding the importance of starting a savings program early. However, you may want to begin with an RRSP rather than a Tax-Free Savings Account because of the tax deduction the former will generate. Take a close look at the two options before you decide.

In either case, you should keep your costs as low as possible at the outset. Normally, I would recommend a self-directed plan for an aggressive young investor. But the annual fee would be out of line with the amount of money you have available. Therefore, I suggest you begin with a no-fee mutual fund plan from one of the financial institutions you have talked to.

My advice is to start with a high-quality balanced fund and put the $2000 into that. Then, as you add more money to the plan, buy other funds for diversification. Once you have $15,000 invested, switch to a self-directed plan at a brokerage firm that will give you more investment options.

TFSAs FOR OLDER PEOPLE

Q I read the first edition of your book on Tax-Free Savings Accounts (TFSAs). Very informative and easy to understand. My question: You gave examples of how couples can become millionaires. Great, but what does a 70-year-old widow do to achieve similar status? I did start a TFSA this year and have investments in mutual funds, GICs, and so on. How do I position myself to get the best results? Thank you for paying attention to those of us who don't want to leave all our money to the governments!

A I wish I could promise that you, too, could become a millionaire with your TFSA, but unless you plan to live until about 110, I really can't. It takes time, especially given the low annual contribution limit.

However, you can use your plan to maximize your tax-exempt investment earnings for as long as you live. The best way to achieve that is to hold securities that you expect to generate the most taxable profit inside your TFSA. These would normally be stocks or mutual funds, especially in a low-interest-rate environment.

Let's say you have a choice between investing in a GIC that pays 2.5 percent and a stock that you expect to gain 10 percent over the next year. For every $1000 invested in the GIC, you would shelter $25 annually in interest. The stock would generate a capital gain of $100 for every $1000 invested. Half of that ($50) would be taxable outside a TFSA. So you double the tax-sheltering value of the plan by holding the stock in the TFSA. Of course, that involves more risk, but your question was how to get the best results.

DOUBLING YOUR TFSA

Q I opened my $5000 TFSA account with one of the banks in January 2009. The interest paid started out at 4 percent and is now reduced to about 1 percent. I do not know where to invest to get the best rates. Could you please give me a few great options from which to choose? One of your readers wrote the following, which I thought was rather amazing: "After making a $5000 contribution to my TFSA this spring, I have managed to build it to $12,000." Thank you.

A Obviously, our reader did not build $5000 into $12,000 by putting his money into a savings account or a GIC. Although he did not tell us how he managed to more than double his TFSA assets in a few months, he probably opened a self-directed plan and invested in stocks when the market was down in early 2009. He didn't have to buy penny mining stocks to do it. An investment of $5000 in Bank of Montreal shares on February 24, 2009, would have been worth $11,350 in early August of that year, not including dividends. There are many other examples of blue-chip stocks more than doubling in that period.

Of course, there is more risk in investing in the stock market. People have to decide for themselves whether they are willing to accept that. If you want to stick with low-risk, interest-bearing investments, the best rates are usually offered by smaller financial institutions. But a word of warning: Before you decide to move your TFSA somewhere else for a slightly higher return, ask whether any transfer or account-closing fees will be charged. They would probably exceed any additional interest you would earn for the next year. And don't expect to double your money any time soon by sticking with a savings account or GIC.

RRSPs and TFSAs

RRSP TRANSFERS

Q Can I transfer funds from my RRSP to a TFSA?

A This question came up many times. The answer is no, and if you think about it for a moment the reason is obvious. RRSP contributions generate a tax deduction. The offset is that you pay tax when the money comes out of the plan. TFSA withdrawals are tax-free. So if you were allowed to shift money from an RRSP to a TFSA, you would end up having a deduction going in but paying no tax coming out. The government may have been in a generous mood when it created TFSAs, but not that generous.

TFSA OR RRSP?

Q Would you say that TFSAs are becoming a better way to invest than RRSPs? I have both, at 62, no dependents and no personal debt. Would bank preferreds go into either one?

A It's not a matter of one being "better" than the other. They're both excellent savings vehicles. Which one should get priority depends on your personal situation.

As a general rule, if you expect your income to be lower after retirement than it is now, contribute to an RRSP first. That's because your tax rate now is higher than it will be after you stop work. Your refund will therefore be greater than the amount of tax you'll be assessed when the money is withdrawn from the plan.

If you expect your income to be higher after retirement (perhaps because of a generous pension plan or an anticipated inheritance that will be invested), then use the TFSA first.

You can put bank preferreds into either plan, provided it is self-directed. However, you will lose the benefit of the dividend tax credit by doing so.

RRSP WITHDRAWAL STRATEGY

Q I am 62 and retired. My taxable income last year was just over $24,000, around $14,000 below the threshold where I would have gone up to the 22 percent income tax bracket from 15 percent. This is actually a two-part question. I have approximately $400,000 in an RRSP that I don't expect to need until I must convert to a RRIF at age 71. Is there a case to be made for withdrawing $5500 from my RRSP and investing the money in a TFSA, or is it better to leave the money in the RRSP until I must withdraw it? My tax accounting is simple enough that I can fairly accurately calculate for tax purposes the monetary difference between the lowest (15 percent) tax bracket and the next higher bracket prior to year-end, if I wanted to withdraw the maximum amount up to the 15 percent threshold. I have enough capital outside my RRSP that I am able to put the allowable $5500 into a TFSA account for the next eight years without using my RRSP money.

A Your last sentence tips the balance here. If you did not have the money available outside the RRSP for a TFSA contribution, I would have said your logic makes sense. But you do, so it doesn't.

The goal of any investor should be to minimize taxes. This means tax-sheltering as much money as you can for as long as you can. The money in the RRSP is already tax-sheltered. The capital outside the plan is not, so you will pay tax at the marginal rate on any investment income it earns.

Therefore, your best strategy is to shelter as much of that capital as possible by using it to make a maximum TFSA contribution each year.

You did not mention a spouse but if you have one you can give him or her $5500 each year to open an individual plan, thereby doubling the tax-sheltered amount.

WHERE TO DRAW MONEY?

Q In the next two to five years, my wife and I will be funding our retirement from CPP/OAS, a small pension, non-sheltered investments, TFSAs, and RRSPs.

For tax efficiency, I assume we should draw down from our non-sheltered investments first (to supplement CPP/OAS and pension income). However, once those funds have been exhausted, will it be more tax efficient to drawn down from the TFSAs or RRSPs first?

We loaded up our TFSAs with blue-chip, dividend-generating equities that should provide a dividend stream and (hopefully) long-term capital gains that can continue to grow completely tax-sheltered in the TFSAs. If these same investments were made in the RRSP, the dividend income and capital gains would eventually be taxed on withdrawal as if they were interest income. But these TFSA benefits will be short-lived if we have to draw down from the TFSAs first (recognizing that our non-sheltered investments will run out in a few years).

A I would leave the money in the TFSAs and draw down the RRSPs. Here's why:

Let's suppose you have a $5000 investment in each plan earning 7 percent annually. Five years from now, that investment will be worth $7,012.76. Now you are faced with a withdrawal decision. If you take the money from the RRSP, using a marginal tax rate of 30 percent, you will be assessed $2,103.83 on the withdrawal. That will leave you with a net after-tax return of $4,908.93. Note that is less than the value of the original $5,000 investment, which means that all the income you earned over the five years and more went in taxes. By comparison, a TFSA withdrawal will be worth the full $7,012.76 – you keep *all* the investment income.

This example does not take into account the benefit of

the tax refund you received for the RRSP contribution, but that is in the past. What you are concerned about now is realizing the highest after-tax return from invested money that is already tax-sheltered. Leaving the TFSAs intact is the best way to do that.

Taxes and TFSAs

WANTS TO CLAIM A LOSS

Q I transferred 600 trust fund units valued at $5000 to my TFSA from a non-registered account. They increased slightly in value and I sold them recently at a considerable loss from my original purchase. Can I still use this capital loss against my capital gains in the non-registered account it was transferred from when filling out my tax return?

A It sounds like you have made a classic and costly mistake. Based on your question, it appears that your units were already in a loss position before you moved them to the TFSA. In that case, you lost the right to claim a capital loss when you transferred them.

With TFSAs, as with RRSPs, the rules are that when an asset is transferred into a plan from a non-registered account, it is deemed to have been sold for tax purposes. Any capital gain is taxable and must be declared on your next return. But, and here is the kicker, capital losses are not recognized in this situation and cannot be claimed. You should have sold the shares instead of transferring them and deposited the proceeds in the TFSA. That would have crystallized the loss for tax purposes. There is nothing you can do now, unfortunately.

FUTURE TAX RATES

Q Where do you feel tax rates will be 10 years in the future compared to the present?

A Talk about crystal-ball gazing! The obvious answer is: Who knows? Most governments in recent years have recognized that lower tax rates encourage higher employment and greater economic activity. Offsetting that are the large deficits that were incurred in creating the stimulus programs to combat the recession. Many economists believe that without tax increases, those deficits will continue for years to come.

On balance, my guess is that governments will first try to close the deficit gap by raising sales taxes. This might be done by extending the harmonized sales tax (HST) to those provinces where it does not already apply, although the British Columbia experience may make that difficult. Alternatively, a future federal government could raise its sales tax rate by a point or two. Higher federal income taxes would be a last resort but can't be ruled out. If they are required, lower- and middle-income wage earners would likely face very small increases with upper-income earners bearing most of the financial burden.

WILL TFSA DIVIDENDS BE TAXED?

Q I have one question: Assume I invest $5000 by buying a bank stock with a good dividend yield. If the stock value is unchanged at year-end but I received some dividend payments giving me a total value in my TFSA account at December 31 of, say, $5200, will I be penalized? I know that if the stock value increases we are okay but do I have to allow for dividend or interest or distribution payments when calculating my maximum?

A No worries. All profits earned inside a Tax-Free Savings Account are tax-free, regardless of their source—capital gains, dividends, or interest. The only way you risk putting yourself in an overcontribution situation is if you deposit more than the allowable maximum per year into the plan.

CLAIMING A CAPITAL LOSS

Q If I sell a stock in an unregistered account and generate a capital loss, can I still claim this capital loss if I immediately repurchase the same stock within a Tax-Free Savings Account?

A No. The "superficial loss" rule would apply. This states that if you, an "affiliated person" or a trust you control, buys the same stock "during the period starting 30 calendar days before the sale and ending 30 calendar days after the sale," no capital loss can be claimed. TFSAs fall under the "trusts" designation. See the Capital Gains Guide published by the Canada Revenue Agency for more details.[4]

U.S. DIVIDENDS

Q I have a question on TFSAs that I have never seen addressed in your many writings on this subject. It relates to using U.S. companies that pay high dividends. I am retired, and my income from my pension and savings results in most of my OAS being clawed back. As a result, I concluded that it is more advantageous for me to hold, for example, AT&T in my Tax-Free Savings Account rather than in an open account in spite of the U.S. withholding tax. Is this assumption correct, or am I missing something?

A You can argue this two ways. On the negative side, dividends from American companies paid into TFSAs are not exempt from the 15 percent U.S. withholding tax, unlike payments made to RRSPs and RRIFs. This is one of the few instances in which TFSAs are not actually tax-free. Plus there is no recourse—you cannot claim a foreign tax credit for tax withheld from payments to a registered plan.

The positive side is that the 15 percent tax is all you will pay. The net dividends can be withdrawn from the TFSA at any time, tax-free. Also, they will not be considered as income, so will have no effect on your susceptibility to the OAS clawback.

Contrast that with an RRSP/RRIF where you'll pay no withholding tax but when the dividends are eventually withdrawn they'll be taxed at your marginal rate, which will probably be much more than 15 percent. Plus, RRSP/RRIF withdrawals are considered regular income for OAS purposes.

In a non-registered account, U.S. dividends would be treated as ordinary income since they do not qualify for the dividend tax credit, so here again you will pay tax at your marginal rate.

The bottom line is that your thinking is correct. You'll pay less tax on those AT&T dividends in a TFSA. But they will not be tax-free.

17

Yes, You Can Be a Millionaire!

TFSAs can make you a millionaire! Not in one year, or five, or even ten. But if you're young enough and stay with the plan, it is certainly an attainable goal. When you combine TFSAs with RRSPs, it's almost a sure thing, providing you can save enough and you invest wisely.

Of course, being a millionaire isn't what it used to be. Fifty years ago, a millionaire was someone who could live like royalty. These days, it's anyone who can afford to drive a car! Well, that's overstating the case, but many families who have mortgage-free homes and some savings put aside are probably getting close to millionaire status.

Nonetheless, the idea of being a millionaire remains a financial dream for many people. TFSAs will make that dream easier to achieve, but you will still need discipline and investment acumen to bring it all together.

In my book *6 Steps to $1 Million*, I wrote that there are two tracks to great wealth. One is to create it through hard work and innovation. The other is to save it. TFSAs are part of the savings track.

Let's look at four fictional couples and see how each might gain millionaire status with TFSAs and how quickly it could happen.

Sean and Alison: Slow and Steady

We'll begin by considering the situation of Sean and Alison, who live in Halifax. Alison inherited the family home after her mother died, so they are living mortgage-free. This enables them to save more than most young people their age.

Both of them had made RRSP contributions in early 2008. They were shocked when they discovered that they had lost 40 percent in the stock market meltdown later that year. After that, they decided "never again." In the future, all their money would be put into safe securities such as GICs. They both understand this will reduce their potential returns, but that is a price they are willing to pay for peace of mind.

Both Sean and Alison opened TFSAs on January 2, 2009, and contributed the $5000 maximum. They were both 25 at the time. The money was invested in five-year GICs. They have done the same thing every year since, and they intend to continue doing so for the foreseeable future, increasing their contributions as the limits rise. Over the years, as interest rates rise and fall, they expect an average annual return of 4 percent.

How long do you think it will take them to accumulate a million dollars between them in their TFSAs at this slow but sure savings rate? Would you believe they will have reached that goal early in 2044, at which time they will be 60 years old? That's right—assuming that inflation runs at 2 percent a year going forward and contribution limits increase as per the existing law, even a low-risk investment program can make a young couple millionaires before their normal retirement age. And remember, all that money is tax-free. This table shows their progress.

How Sean and Alison's TFSAs Grow

Years	Contribution limit (per person)	Period-end TFSA value (combined)
2009–2012	$5000	$44,163
2013–2016	$5500	$100,244
2017–2021	$6000	$189,558
2022–2025	$6500	$279,168
2026–2028	$7000	$359,477
2029–2031	$7500	$453,059
2032–2035	$8000	$600,677
2036–2038	$8500	$730,869
2039–2040	$9000	$828,697
2041–2043	$9500	$993,854

Assumptions: Maximum contributions are made at start of year. Inflation rate is 2 percent. Average annual return is 4 percent.

Anil and Sujata: Buying Blue Chips

Anil and Sujata live in Regina. He was 43 and she was 42 in 2009. They have two children, both of whom are now living away from home. They jointly run a successful hardware store. Their mortgage is paid off. However, the cost of raising a family and paying for their house has left them with no retirement savings. Now they want to remedy that.

Because they had no investments, they weren't hurt by the market collapses of 2002 and 2008. But many of their friends were. They don't want the same thing to happen to them, but they also realize that because they have no money put aside for retirement and they have a relatively short time frame, they will have to take more risk if they are going to be able to sell the business and retire when Anil reaches 65.

Together, they decide that, considering the circumstances, the best strategy is to use their TFSAs to invest in a portfolio of blue-chip stocks. They realize that the markets will continue to fluctuate over the years, but they believe that by dollar-cost averaging their investments over a long period of time, they will be able to achieve an average annual compound rate of return of 8 percent, including dividends. They started as soon as TFSAs became available in 2009. Can they achieve their million-dollar objective by 2031? Let's take a look.

How Anil and Sujata's TFSAs Grow

Years	Contribution limit (per person)	Period-end TFSA value (combined)
2009–2012	$5000	$48,666
2013–2016	$5500	$119,742
2017–2021	$6000	$251,972
2022–2025	$6500	$406,071
2026–2028	$7000	$560,617
2029–2031	$7500	$758,808
2032–2034	$8000	$1,011,978

Assumptions: Maximum contributions are made at start of year. Inflation rate is 2%. Average annual return is 8%.

The answer is, not quite. Under these assumptions, their combined plans will be worth about $760,000 in 2031. But if they continue on the same course for another three years until 2034, when Anil will be 68, they'll achieve the million-dollar plateau.

Of course, if they save money in an RRSP as well, they'll reach a million dollars easily, and much sooner. If they each contribute $10,000 a year to an RRSP (assuming they have enough earned income to do so), their plans will be worth almost $990,000 after 20 years, again assuming 8 percent annual growth. Add that to the TFSAs and they are well beyond the million-dollar mark. And here's the kicker: If their marginal tax rate is 35 percent, their RRSP contributions will generate tax refunds of $3500 each (or $7000 for the two of them), which will cover a large portion of the TFSA contributions. This is a good way to make both plans work in tandem.

David and Rebecca: Rolling the Dice

David is a stockbroker and Rebecca is a chartered accountant. They are both very savvy about money and investing, and they are determined to get as rich as possible as quickly as they can. They understand the risk involved, but because they don't plan to have children, they are prepared to live with that. In 2009, David was 32 and Rebecca was 30. They live in Montreal.

David knows all the tricks of the brokerage trade. He knows how to use options, how to leverage investments through exchange-traded funds, and how to play market cycles. He understands the investment rules governing TFSAs and is convinced he can operate within them to generate an average annual return of 15 percent on their money. A target this high is extremely aggressive and requires active management of the account and a lot of intestinal fortitude. David believes he can do it, and Rebecca supports him.

They decide they are going to push their TFSAs to the limit in their investment choices. He reviews the portfolios at least once a day, buying and selling regularly. He buys energy stocks when oil is cheap and sells when crude spikes higher. He trades in and out of gold shares. He buys exchange-traded funds that pay off double when the indexes they track move in the right direction.

Most of the time, it works. Like all investors, David suffers some setbacks along the way, but they are more than offset by years in which he is able to double the money in the plans. Over time, he achieves his 15 percent average annual goal. So let's see how much money David and Rebecca end up with.

How David and Rebecca's TFSAs Grow

Years	Contribution limit (per person)	Period-end TFSA value (combined)
2009–2012	$5000	$57,424
2013–2016	$5500	$163,601
2017–2021	$6000	$422,105
2022–2025	$6500	$812,914
2026–2028	$7000	$1,292,248
2029–2031	$7500	$2,025,249
2032–2035	$8000	$3,634,051
2036–2038	$8500	$5,594,825

Assumptions: Maximum contributions are made at start of year. Inflation rate is 2%. Average annual return is 15%.

By the time David turns 50 in 2027, their combined TFSAs will have passed the million-dollar level, but he's just getting started. Compounding works like a snowball rolling downhill, rapidly increasing your savings in size as it goes. It takes only an additional four years or so to add another million to the pot. By the time he is 61 and Rebecca is 59, their TFSAs have accumulated almost $5.6 million, all tax-free. They'll be able to retire very comfortably on that money, although David will probably want to keep going. He's the type you'll see in the library of a cruise ship, following the markets via satellite internet as he and Rebecca tour the world.

Jenny and Paul: Small Savings Add Up

Of course, many families will not be able to put aside enough money to make a maximum TFSA contribution. The budget is stretched thin just keeping up with household expenses; there's hardly anything left over at the end of the month.

Jenny and Paul were in that position in 2009. At that time the then 22-year-old Winnipeg couple was living common law, although they married two years later. They both work at modest-paying jobs, she as a library assistant and he as a bus driver. They have no children but intend to start a family someday.

They liked the idea of opening TFSAs, but they realized that they wouldn't be able to contribute much, at least at the start. So they made a deal. They began by putting $1000 a year each into their plans. Every five years, they would add another $500 each to the amount. They decided to invest the money in balanced mutual funds, which they hope will return an average of 7 percent annually. Here's what happens as the years pass.

How Jenny and Paul's TFSAs Grow

Years	Contribution limit (per person)	Period-end TFSA value (combined)
2009–2013	$1000	$12,307
2014–2018	$1500	$35,720
2019–2023	$2000	$74,713
2024–2028	$2500	$135,555
2029–2033	$3000	$227,043
2034–2038	$3500	$361,513
2039–2043	$4000	$566,267
2044–2048	$4500	$835,572
2049–2053	$5000	$1,233,466

Assumptions: Contributions are made at start of year. Inflation rate is 2%. Average annual return is 7%.

This one is an eye-opener! Even starting with very modest contributions and investing in moderate-risk balanced funds, Jenny and Paul are able to build their combined TFSAs to a value of more than a million dollars by the time they are 65 (the actual amount in the plans at the end of the year in which they celebrate their 65th birthdays will be $1,142,772). So even young people who don't have a lot of money can use these plans to create significant personal wealth if they are willing to make the commitment.

If you want to check out how TFSAs can work most effectively for your family, Scotiabank has created a useful online calculator that demonstrates how quickly your tax-free savings will grow. You can plug in any assumptions you wish, including initial lump-sum contributions, monthly contributions, various rates of return, and time horizons. It's available at www.scotiabank.com/tfsatool.

A Tax-Free Future?

Tax-Free Savings Accounts were really created out of political expediency. As we saw in Chapter 1, Finance Minister Jim Flaherty had painted himself into a corner when it came to presenting his 2008 budget. Having given away everything that was left in the store in his Economic Statement the previous October, he badly needed something to showcase in February after the anticipated election failed to materialize. TFSAs fit the bill and the immediate cost to the Treasury was minimal.

As it turned out, no one gave the Conservatives much credit for TFSAs in the election campaign that took place in the fall of 2008; in fact, they were barely mentioned. But now they're here, and at some time in the future another finance minister may look back and ask, "Why?"

As the years pass, the amount of money invested in TFSAs will reach hundreds of billions of dollars. Some economists are already predicting that the time will come when many older Canadians will pay no taxes at all while at the same time drawing heavily on government programs such as Old Age Security and medicare.

Whether this will be sustainable is something that future governments will have to decide. It is not inconceivable that, at some point, we may see a freeze on TFSA contributions or a tax on the withdrawal of investment earnings, albeit at a reduced rate.

But all of that is problematic, and if any changes are made to the system, it won't happen for many years. For now, Canadians have an extremely valuable savings program with which to build their personal fortunes. Make the most of it!

ACTION SUMMARY

1. Make your TFSA contributions at the start of each year to maximize tax-sheltered growth.
2. Decide on an investment strategy that suits your temperament and financial knowledge. Even a low-risk approach will enable a couple to accumulate a million dollars in their plans if they have enough time.
3. You don't have to be well off to build wealth in a TFSA. Even if your income is modest, open an account and keep adding to it. Remember, the original reason why the C.D. Howe Institute promoted these plans was that they are an effective savings option for lower-income people. The younger you are when you start, the more effectively they'll work for you over time.

18

How Much
Have You Learned?

Okay, it's exam time. You've made the effort to get through
this book so you are obviously committed to learning how to
use your Tax-Free Savings Account to obtain the best possible
results. Now try these two tests to see just how much you
know. You should score at least 80 percent on the first one.
The second is much harder so a passing grade is 65 percent.
The answers are at the end of each section.

Test #1 – The Easy Stuff

1. What year were TFSAs launched?
   a) 2001
   b) 2008
   c) 2009
   d) 2012

2. The annual contribution limit per person until 2012
   was how much?
   a) $2000
   b) $5000
   c) $5500
   d) $10,000

3. You can claim a tax deduction for a TFSA contribution.
   a) True
   b) False

4. How old do you have to be to open a TFSA?
   a) 16
   b) 18
   c) 21
   d) There is no minimum age.

5. If I don't contribute this year, I can make it up next year.
   a) True
   b) False

6. At what age must you terminate a TFSA?
   a) 69
   b) 71
   c) 75
   d) There is no age limit.

7. You can loan your spouse/partner money to open a TFSA with no penalty.
   a) True
   b) False

8. If you borrow money to invest in a TFSA, the interest is tax-deductible.
   a) True
   b) False

9. TFSA withdrawals are not considered as income for purposes of calculating Guaranteed Income Supplement benefits.
   a) True
   b) False

10. What is the maximum number of plans permitted to each person?
    a) One
    b) Two
    c) Five
    d) There is no limit.

11. If you withdraw money from your TFSA, the amount is added to the next year's contribution limit.
    a) True
    b) False

12. Use an RRSP instead of a TFSA if you expect your income to be higher after you retire.
    a) True
    b) False

13. A self-directed TFSA is the least expensive type of plan.
    a) True
    b) False

14. You are allowed to have both a TFSA and an RRSP.
    a) True
    b) False

15. When the last surviving spouse dies, all the money in a TFSA can pass to the children tax-free.
    a) True
    b) False

ANSWERS

1. c	6. d	11. a
2. b	7. a	12. b
3. b	8. b	13. b
4. b	9. a	14. a
5. a	10. d	15. a

Test #2 – The Expert Level

1. Which of the following is not eligible for a TFSA?
   a) Stocks
   b) Bonds
   c) Real estate
   d) All of the above

2. You can transfer money directly from an RRSP to a TFSA.
   a) True
   b) False

3. Your TFSA holds a locked-in GIC. You desperately need cash. You can use the TFSA as collateral for a loan at your bank.
   a) True
   b) False

4. I can open a TFSA for my spouse/partner and contribute to it.
   a) True
   b) False

5. I own mutual fund units that have lost money. I can transfer them to my TFSA and claim a capital loss on my tax return.
   a) True
   b) False

6. Swaps are permitted in TFSAs.
   a) True
   b) False

7. In all provinces and territories except one you should name your spouse/partner as the successor holder. Which one is the exception?
   a) Nova Scotia
   b) Yukon
   c) Quebec
   d) Alberta

8. Mutual fund investments made through a bank TFSA
   are eligible for deposit insurance.
   a) True
   b) False

9. The 15-percent withholding tax on U.S.-source
   dividends does not apply to TFSAs. The dividends are
   received tax-free.
   a) True
   b) False

10. Shares in small businesses may be held in TFSAs.
    a) True
    b) False

11. How much is the penalty for an inadvertent
    overcontribution?
    a) $100
    b) 1 percent per month
    c) 10 percent per year
    d) The amount is at the discretion of the CRA.

12. Using the Rule of 72, how long will it take a $1000
    TFSA contribution to double if the average annual
    compound rate of return is 6 percent?
    a) Six years
    b) Eight years
    c) Twelve years
    d) Fifteen years

13. Which of the following should not be given a high priority when setting up a TFSA to be used as an emergency fund?
    a) Safety
    b) A high return
    c) Low fees
    d) Liquidity

14. If you emigrate from Canada permanently, it's generally a good idea to close your TFSA before leaving.
    a) True
    b) False

15. If you don't have the cash available, you are allowed to make a contribution in kind to a TFSA.
    a) True
    b) False

ANSWERS

1. c	6. b	11. b
2. b	7. c	12. c
3. a	8. b	13. b
4. b	9. b	14. a
5. b	10. a	15. a

For More Investment Information

Retirement's Harsh New Realities

In this hard-hitting book, Gordon Pape pulls no punches in explaining the realities of retirement that confront Canadians, including collapsing pension plans, government inertia, a tax system that works against older people, pitiful savings rates, and the fact that there are no safe investments. And this is just the beginning, he writes. We are about to experience a series of wrenching changes in our retirement system as governments, corporations, and individuals struggle to cope with a tidal wave of harsh economic, demographic, and social realities.

But, as he puts it, "there are solutions to all problems" and this book offers them. Pape shares his common sense advice to help readers understand the realities of retirement and offers sound, practical solutions for protecting your family's future in a rapidly changing world. Inside you'll find advice on

- Why a demographic crisis is creating widespread social unrest
- The Baby Boomer retirement crunch and what it means

- The failing pension system and what to do about it
- How to benefit from RRSPs and TFSAs
- Tips for reducing the tax hit
- How to succeed in today's turbulent investment climate
- Avoiding the crisis: how to protect your future

Despite the harsh new realities, Pape provides workable solutions to every problem. If it's not already, retirement planning must become one of your life's priorities.

Money Savvy Kids

Most of us grew up knowing very little about money and how to manage it. The result is the most indebted generation in Canadian history. Don't let your children make the same mistakes. This fun-to-read book by Gordon Pape and his daughter, Deborah Kerbel, will help get them, and you, on the right track. It contains sound practical information from Canada's most trusted financial writer plus many delightful and sometimes hilarious personal anecdotes and children's quotes that will leave you laughing while you learn. Some highlights:

- How to teach the "value" of money
- Are allowances a good idea and, if so, how much?
- Saving, spending, and sharing
- Teaching your kids to shop smart
- Coping with children-directed advertising

- Games that teach money skills
- Great websites and apps—some reviewed by the kids themselves
- Money-smart books for young readers
- Saving for college

This book is a must-read for all parents with children between the ages of five and seventeen. Don't miss it.

Newsletters

Gordon Pape is the editor and publisher of these investment newsletters.

Internet Wealth Builder. This weekly email newsletter covers all aspects of investing and money management, including stocks, bonds, mutual funds, income trusts, taxes, and general economic comment. The seasoned team of contributing editors includes some of Canada's best investment minds. The newsletter takes a conservative approach to money management and was among the first to warn of the drop in the Toronto Stock Exchange in a lead article published in mid-June 2008, just a few days after the TSX hit an all-time high. Since then, it has recommended many securities that have earned large profits for its readers.

The Income Investor. This twice-monthly newsletter focuses on income-generating securities with the goal of providing readers with above-average returns consistent with reasonable risk. At a time when interest rates are low and income trusts have been virtually phased out of existence, the guidance provided by this letter is vital to anyone seeking steady cash flow from their investments.

For more information on these newsletters, visit www. BuildingWealth.ca or call toll-free 1-888-287-8229.

Website

More financial information from Gordon Pape can be found at www.BuildingWealth.ca. The site offers free investment articles, a Q&A feature, valuable free budget and net worth spreadsheets, book excerpts, and more.

Notes

1: THE BEGINNING: BUDGET 2008

1. The Honourable James M. Flaherty, P.C., M.P., minister of finance, *The Budget Speech 2008*, Department of Finance Canada, February 26, 2008. Available at www.budget. gc.ca/2008/speech-discours/speech-discours-eng.html.
2. Ibid.
3. Julie Smyth, "Budget Report Card," *National Post*, February 26, 2008.
4. Benjamin Tal, "The New Tax-Free Savings Account: How Popular Will It Be?" *Consumer Watch Canada*, CIBC World Markets, September 11, 2008.
5. Steven Chase, "Small Change for Tighter Times," *The Globe and Mail*, February 27, 2008.
6. Rob Carrick, "A Place to Park Cash but Not the Break They Promised," *The Globe and Mail*, February 27, 2008.

2: SOME HISTORY

1. Department of Finance, *The Budget Plan 2004*, Annex 9. Available at www.fin.gc.ca/budget04/pdf/bp2004e.pdf.
2. "What Constrains Flaherty's Budget," *The Globe and Mail*, February 18, 2008.
3. William B.P. Robson and Finn Poschmann, *Steering Through Turbulence: The Shadow Federal Budget for 2008*, C.D. Howe Institute, February 2008. Available at www.cdhowe.org/pdf/ backgrounder_111.pdf.

4. Conservative Party of Canada, *Platform 2004, Demanding Better*.

5. Conservative Party of Canada, *Platform 2006, Stand Up for Canada*. Available at www.scribd.com/doc/334166/ Conservative-Party-of-Canada-Federal-Election-Platform-2006.

6. HM Revenue and Customs, *ISA Rules Are Changing*. Available at www.hmrc.gov.uk/ISA/rule-change-april08.htm.

7. HM Revenue and Customs, *ISA Bulletin*, Number 14–25, June 2009. Available at www.hmrc.gov.uk/isa/bulletin14.htm.

8. Richard Shillington, *New Poverty Traps: Means Testing and Modest-Income Seniors*, C.D. Howe Institute, April 2003. Available at www.cdhowe.org/pdf/backgrounder_65.pdf.

9. Finn Poschmann and William B.P. Robson, *Saving's Grace: A Framework to Promote Financial Independence for Low-Income Canadians*, C.D. Howe Institute, November 2004. Available at www.cdhowe.org/pdf/backgrounder_86.pdf.

10. John Stapleton and Richard Shillington, *No Strings Attached: How the Tax-Free Savings Account Can Help Lower-Income Canadians Get Ahead*, C.D. Howe Institute, September 2008. Available at www.cdhowe.org/pdf/ebrief_64.pdf.

11. James Pierlot and Alex Laurin, *Pooled Registered Pension Plans: Pension Savior—Or A New Tax on the Poor?* C.D. Howe Institute, August 2012. Available at www.cdhowe.org/pdf/ Commentary_359.pdf.

3: THE BASIC RULES

1. Survey, Polls & Research, "Scotiabank Study Confirms Canadians Seek More Information on the Tax Free Savings Account," November 6, 2008.

2. Richard Shillington, *New Poverty Traps: Means Testing and Modest-Income Seniors*, C.D. Howe Institute, April 2003. Available at www.cdhowe.org/pdf/backgrounder_65.pdf.

3. Mackenzie Financial Corporation, *Tax and Estate Planning Team: Investor Guide: Tax-Free Savings Accounts (TFSAs)*. Available at www.mackenziefinancial.com/en/pub/products/accouns/tfsa/tfsa_resources.shtml.

5: RAINY DAY TFSAs
1. Statistics Canada.

6: TFSAs OR RRSPs: WHICH TO CHOOSE?
1. Department of Finance Canada, *The Budget Plan 2008*, Annex 4. Available at www.budget.gc.ca/2008/plan/ann4a-eng.html.
2. C.D. Howe Institute. Available at www.cdhowe.org/pdf/ebrief_91.pdf.
3. *Pension Benefits Guaranty Corporation Annual Report*. Available at www.pbgc.gov/res/reports/ar2011.html.
4. James Daw, "Teachers Take Pension Cutback," *Toronto Star*, October 1, 2008. Available at www.thestar.com/Business/article/509241.
5. Richard Shillington, *New Poverty Traps: Means Testing and Modest-Income Seniors*, C.D. Howe Institute, April 2003. Available at www.cdhowe.org/pdf/backgrounder_65.pdf.

7: TAX RELIEF FOR SENIORS
1. Canada Revenue Agency, *2012 Preliminary Statistics (2010 Tax Year)*, Table 4. Available at www.cra-arc.gc.ca/gncy/stts/gb10/pst/ntrm/pdf/table4-eng.pdf.
2. Statistics Canada, 2007/2009. Available at www.statcan.gc.ca/tables-tableaux/sum-som/l01/cst01/health72a-eng.htm.

8: EDUCATION SAVINGS
1. A.J.C. King and W.K. Warren, *Transition to College: Perspectives of Secondary School Students*, Social Program Evaluation Group, Faculty of Education, Queen's University, 2006.

9: SAVE TAXES BY SPLITTING INCOME

1. Ernst & Young, *2012 Personal Tax Calculator*. Available at www.ey.com/CA/en/Services/Tax/Tax-Calculators-2009-Personal-Tax.
2. Department of Finance Canada, *The Budget Plan 2008*, Annex 4. Available at www.budget.gc.ca/2008/plan/ann4a-eng.html.

10: PASSING ON

1. Ernst & Young, *2012 Personal Tax Calculator*. Available at www.ey.com/CA/en/Services/Tax/Tax-Calculators-2012-Personal-Tax.
2. Canada Revenue Agency, *Tax-Free Savings Account (TFSA), Guide for Individuals*. Available at www.cra-arc.gc.ca/E/pub/tg/rc4466/README.html.

11: TAX-SAVING STRATEGIES

1. To illustrate, suppose you buy a mutual fund at $10 a unit and receive an ROC distribution of $0.40. Your ACB will be $9.60 ($10 − $0.40 = $9.60).
2. Rates as per 2012 tax year. In the 2008 budget, the federal government announced it will reduce the amount of the gross-up and the tax-credit percentage in three stages from 2010–2012 to reflect reductions in the corporate tax rate.

12: SPECIAL SITUATIONS

1. Tax Specialist Group. Available at www.taxspecialistgroup.ca/public/taxtips.asp?n=11-08&site=tsg.

16: YOUR TFSA QUESTIONS

1. Department of Finance Canada, *The Budget Plan 2008*, Annex 4, Attribution Rules. Available at www.budget.gc.ca/2008/plan/ann4a-eng.html.

2. Canada Revenue Agency, *Who can open a TFSA?* Available at www.cra-arc.gc.ca/tx/ndvdls/tpcs/tfsa-celi/lgbl-eng.html.

3. Canada Revenue Agency, Interpretation Bulletin IT-221R3, *Determination of an Individual's Residence Status.* Available at www.cra-arc.gc.ca/E/pub/tp/it221r3-consolid/it221r3-consolid-e.pdf.

4. Canada Revenue Agency, *Capital Gains Guide 2011.* Available at www.cra-arc.gc.ca/E/pub/tg/t4037/t4037-11e.pdf.

Acknowledgments

Several people provided invaluable assistance in the preparation of this book and the two editions that preceded it. When the first edition was published in 2009, the whole concept of TFSAs was still very new, and many of the nuances of these plans were not well understood. I asked several experts in the field of tax and personal finance to assist me in sorting out the intricacies of these plans, and they were very generous in sharing their knowledge.

Even now, with TFSAs entering their fifth year at the start of 2013, there are subtleties relating to the program that are open to professional interpretation. These have been dealt with in this latest edition, again with the assistance of some of the top professionals in the field.

I would especially like to acknowledge the contributions made by the following:

Wilmot George, director, Tax and Estate Planning, Mackenzie Financial

Jason Enouy, senior manager, Process & Regulatory Solutions, Scotiabank Wealth Management

Jamie Golombek, managing director, Tax and Estate Planning, CIBC Private Wealth Management

Gena Katz, executive director, Tax Practice, Ernst & Young

William B.P. Robson, president and CEO, C.D. Howe Institute

Finn Poschmann, vice-president, Research, C.D. Howe Institute

Evelyn Jacks, president, The Knowledge Bureau

I would also like to thank the staff of the federal Department of Finance and the Canada Revenue Agency who handled all my queries and followed up with the answers in time to meet my tight deadlines. The people in our public service don't get enough recognition for efforts such as this, so I'm taking this opportunity to say a heartfelt "thank you."

Special thanks to my chief researcher (and daughter), Kim Pape-Green, who also prepared the endnotes and the index.

Of course, this book would not have been possible without the support and encouragement of my long-time editor, Andrea Magyar, and her team at Penguin Group Canada. Special thanks also to production editor Sandra Tooze and my copy editor, Patricia Jones.

All these people worked together as a team to make this book possible. No writer can function without them. Thank you.

Index